THE
RULING
CLASS

THE

RULING

CLASS

HOW THEY CORRUPTED AMERICA AND WHAT WE CAN DO ABOUT IT

ANGELO M. CODEVILLA

An American Spectator Book

BEAUFORT
BOOKS

Library of Congress Cataloging-in-Publication Data
Codevilla, Angelo M.
  The ruling class : how political elites hijacked America / Angelo M. Codevilla.
      p. cm.
  "An American Spectator Book."
  Includes bibliographical references.
  ISBN 978-0-8253-0558-0 (alk. paper)
  1. Power (Social sciences)—United States. 2. Elite (Social sciences)—Political activity—United States. 3. United States—Politics and government. I. Title.

JK275.C64 2010
305.5'240973--dc22

                                    2010033483

For inquiries about volume orders, please contact:

Beaufort Books
27 West 20th Street, Suite 1102
New York, NY 10011
sales@beaufortbooks.com

Published in the United States by Beaufort Books
www.beaufortbooks.com

Distributed by Midpoint Trade Books
www.midpointtrade.com

Interior design by Neuwirth & Associates, Inc.

10 9 8 7 6 5 4 3 2 1

Printed in the United States of America

CONTENTS

All men are created equal . . .
The Declaration of Independence, 1776

Who the hell do they think they are?
Heard on the street, 2010

INTRODUCTION

I WAS SHOPPING for antiques once in Paris, just for the hell of it, and I picked up on a sales technique the locals use. I was looking at a supposed relic from the regime of Louis the "Fow-teenth," and a dealer informed me, "This is an important piece."

I asked him, "What's important about it?"

The dealer was clearly not used to being challenged. "Well, it's just an important piece," he finally said.

I recognized it as a scam. "It's important," I wondered. "Important to whom?" He was trying to inflate the price and stroke my ego, and it didn't work.

Because of that incident, I very seldom use the word "important." But nobody had to tell me that Angelo Codevilla's essay, "America's Ruling Class and the Perils of Revolution," is important.

A shorter version of this booklet that you hold in your possibly nicotine-stained hands first ran in the July–August issue of *The American Spectator*. As I reminded my producer Bo Snerdley, it took up eighteen pages. I couldn't spend my entire show reading from it. But the essay is so good, so timely, so thorough and complete, that I had to try anyway.

One reason it appealed to me is that it dovetails with something I have been struggling to explain for twenty years. It's come to a head now with the election of Barack Obama.

For twenty years I have been asked, "Rush, why don't the Republicans do X?" One answer I've settled on is that people never really get out of high school. Wanting to be part of the big clique dominates their lives. It's a quest for power, for acceptance, for belonging to the "in" crowd, however it's defined.

Republicans are the way they are in Washington because Washington is a culture and a place that is run and dominated—not just politically, but socially—by Democrats, by the left. They're the big clique. The Republicans also live there. Everybody wants to get along with those you live next to, and in Washington, the center of power in the world, everybody wants to be in the Ruling Class.

The Ruling Class is the subject of this wonderfully written and crafted essay by Codevilla, who is a professor emeritus at Boston University. We belong to what Professor Codevilla calls the Country Class, meaning not the hick class, but the country.

We are the country. The Ruling Class is a minority. Fewer than 15 percent of Americans agree with the thought process, philosophies, goals, and objectives of the Ruling Class.

We in the Country Class, we believe in merit. We rise or fall based on merit. We believe that a good GPA is what's necessary to get you into college. We believe that performing well on the job is how you get promoted and how you get paid well. That is not true for the Ruling Class. In fact, for them, merit is looked down upon.

As Professor Codevilla points out, these people are a minority, and they have no relationship to the rest of us in the Country Class. Yet somehow we are now being ruled—not governed—by these people.

They have certain strange beliefs. One of these is that the United States is the problem in the world. Another is that those of us not in the Ruling Class haven't got the smarts to know what's best for ourselves. They think they have to decide for us. These are people like Obama and Steve Rattner. They bought up Chrysler and GM and ordered all these dealerships closed under the guise of saving money or saving the auto industry, when in fact what they did was put a whole bunch of people out of work, and in the process shut down a lot of economic activity in the communities where these dealerships were.

These people are threatened by the private sector. They couldn't compete with the average successful person in the private sector. Yet they have the gall to portray themselves as better than us, better than everybody else, more qualified to understand what's best for us.

That's why we need them in charge of our healthcare. That's why we need them in charge of our salt intake, of our trans fat intake, of the obesity of our children. That's why they're talking about dinners now being served in schools, because parents simply aren't responsible enough to feed their kids right, otherwise they'll become fat slobs and put a strain on the American healthcare system.

This is an insidious bunch of people.

But the Ruling Class has a fear. They know that they are a minority, and they know that their time is coming. They know that their Ruling Class status can't be sustained. It hasn't been, throughout history. There have always been revolutions.

In this essay, Professor Codevilla touches on what happens next. He points out that the Ruling Class of today is far more discriminatory and punishing than

King George was of the Colonists in the days of their Revolution. The Tea Party is the modern equivalent of our founding revolutionaries. But how do they pull it off this time?

Professor Codevilla points out that the Tea Party needs a political party. The Tea Party needs a political mechanism in order to revolt and replace the Ruling Class. And if it's the Republican Party—well, I won't try to paraphrase what Professor Codevilla says. But you can imagine, and I encourage you to read his essay now. Because, folks, it's a brilliant piece, and it's important. It's not often that I say that.

—*Rush Limbaugh*

FOREWORD

THIS IS NOT another book about the political-social issues of our time. It offers no recommendations for legislators, executives, or judges on any "hot button" matter. Rather, it is a book about the massive fact that underlies all these issues and makes each a battlefield on which vie partisans of radically different Americas. It is about the fact that America now divides ever more sharply into two classes, the smaller of which holds the commanding heights of government, from which it disposes in ever greater detail of America's economic energies, from which it ordains new ways of living as if it had the right to do so, and from which it asserts that that right is based on the majority class' stupidity, racism, and violent tendencies.

The other class' position is analogous to that of the frog that awoke to the fact that it was being slow-boiled only when getting out of the pan would require perhaps more strength and judgment than it had left. Political clashes over individual issues are so bitter because each represents the attempt of the Ruling Class to lock down the controls already established on its subordinates, and what the subordinates feel may be their last chance to escape.

Why do three out of four Americans believe that our country is heading in the wrong direction, and only one out of five believe that the government is likelier to do good than harm? Vice President Joseph Biden and the editors of the *New York Times* have explained that we are incapable of realizing how much good our government does us because economic dislocation makes us anxious and irritable. Why do so many Americans trust in God and in what they can do for themselves rather than in the government? Barack Obama said that limited economic prospects and narrow social horizons produce "bitter" Americans who "cling to guns or religion or antipathy to people who aren't like us," or to their families. If so, America's founders' self-evident truth that "all men are created equal" must have been wrong. If our current leaders are correct, the American people's opinions result not from mental processes equal to their own, but rather from socioeconomic anxieties plus racist prejudices. This, said Obama, is "something everybody knows is true."

"Everybody"? Certainly for Barack Obama's peers,

for those who see the world through the *New York Times'* lens, for most who run our government at the federal and state level, it is self-evidently true that people whom they consider "downscale" are intellectually and socially incapable of understanding our "complex world." That is why they believe not only that government and what used to be called "public affairs" are both best left to "professionals," but that more and more of what ordinary people think of as private decisions that concern medical care, the use of energy and water, even the consumption of food, should occur within guidelines firmly set by experts like themselves.

Ever since the 1930s, as people who think this way have taken over more and more functions in an ever bigger government, they have become ever more inclined to dismiss the public's opposition as ignorant, and to believe themselves entitled to shape a new and different America. Through their conception of their own superiority, and by accumulating power, they have made themselves into a bipartisan Ruling Class that now dominates public affairs and encroaches ever more into our lives' most intimate details.

This is why millions of Americans are now reasserting our right to obey the Constitution to which officials swear allegiance upon taking office, rather than to obey any official. The most obvious evidence of the American people's desire to be responsible for our own lives and to govern ourselves is the Taxed Enough Already (TEA) Party movement. But that desire transcends all organizations, joining Independents, Republicans, and not a few Democrats into what we might call the Country Party. This party does not have and may never have an organization. Ancient and ubiquitous is the division between the Ins, who benefit from closeness to the king's court, and the Outs in the rest of the country, who must pay for the king's largesse. Like countless others, America's Country Party is the party of the Outs. But there is a difference: America's Outs—the two-thirds of Americans who feel that the Ruling Class is demeaning us, impoverishing us, and demoralizing us—are the people who embody the ideas and habits that made America the world's envy. And they want the Ruling Class off America's back.

The Democratic Party represents the Ruling Class well: A majority of people who vote Democrat tell pollsters that they feel represented by the officials they elect. But only a fourth of Republican voters feel represented by Republican officials. This means that many, if not most, Republican officials are in an untenable position, with their hearts and personal hopes pushing further into the Ruling Class, and their roots withering among their voters. Most of these voters, along with Independents (and a few Democrats), make up the vast Country Party. Sooner rather than later, for better or worse, this supermajority of Americans will get its own political vehicle, either an obviously reformed Republican Party, or a new one. The Tea Party movement is part of the soil in which it must root.

From Atlanta to Seattle, today's Ruling Class was exposed to a narrow, uniform set of ideas, and adopted a set of habits and tastes, as well as a secular canon of sacred myths, saints, sins, and ritual language. The class' chief pretension is its intellectual superiority: its members claim to know things that the common herd cannot. It confuses its own opinions with "science." While most Americans pray to the God who created us in His own image, our Ruling Class prays to themselves as saviors of the planet and as shapers of mankind in *their* own image. While the Ruling Class thinks that Americans are unfit to run their own lives, most Americans have noticed that our Ruling Class has lost every war it has fought, run up an unpayable national debt, and generally made life worse.

* * *

The issues between the two touch every part of our lives. The Ruling Class has gone a long way toward imposing crony capitalism on America. It is now less profitable to serve customers or do a good job than to be invited to help write government rules, to advise on government grants, or to belong to a government-affiliated union. Trading economic privilege for political support is standard in most of the world. America used to be different, but it is becoming less so. The Ruling Class is giving greater and greater power to administrative agencies to make and enforce the rules by which we live. If it has its way, bureaucrats will decide how much energy each of us can use, the quality and quantity of the showers we can take, how many calories we can eat, and whether and what kind of colonoscopy we are given. As voters, we become less and less relevant. The letter of the laws and the Constitution itself are becoming subordinate to the willful reading of same by those in power. Again, this is standard in most of the world, but America used to be exceptional.

Because any standard of right and wrong beyond the Ruling Class' reach challenges its self-conception, its greatest concern has been to denigrate the American people's devotion to God, because the Ruling Class accepts no standard it cannot control. Because natural families represent affections into which government has difficulty intruding, and because natural families educate the children they produce, the Ruling Class has done its best to undermine marriage and to take as much authority from parents as it can.

Hence, the more that an idea or scheme—whether global warming or government-guaranteed medical care—is dear to the Ruling Class, the more the Country Class has turned its back on it. In doing so, the Country Class is rejecting the ideas' patrons just as much as their substance. In short, the Ruling Class has lost the American people's respect. And having responded by insulting the American people, the Ruling Class has denied itself the possibility of ever regaining it. Hence, doing away with the Ruling Class' power and perquisites is the prerequisite for saving America's prosperity, civility, and morality.

Because removing the Democratic Party from positions of power is necessarily the Country Party's immediate objective, it has no choice *in the short run* but to channel most of its electoral energies through the Republican Party. But getting non-Democrat majorities in Congress and state Houses is the easy part. Such majorities will surely be tempted to try to impose on America the reverse of the "revolution from above" that the Ruling Class has inflicted on us. Yet the American people do not want partisan government. They want *self*-governance. That means putting government power in the hands of elected officials rather than bureaucrats—for example, either dismantling administrative agencies or electing their members. For elections to be meaningful, however, citizens would have to take much more responsibility for knowing the issues and keeping officials honest than they have lately exercised.

It is even more essential to self-governance that citizens de-professionalize government by holding elective offices themselves. No legislation would restore parent control over education as much as allowing each neighborhood to administer its school. This would require breaking America's school districts into as many units as needed. This and other measures to restore citizens' control of their lives would be truly revolutionary, because every elected non-professional who sits on a school board or a county commission would be a physical re-affirmation of the basic, self-evident truth on which America was founded: "All men are created equal." In sum, by taking so much power into its self-selected circles, the Ruling Class has gone a long way toward destroying the habits of Americans for economic self-reliance, for citizenship, for family life, and for reverence. Ousting the Ruling Class will not be so difficult or important as reclaiming the habits that made us Americans.

THE

RULING

CLASS

CHAPTER 1

Division, Longstanding and Deep

"Americans are flagrantly ill-informed . . . a nation of dodos."

— JOE KLEIN,
Time magazine, January 25, 2010

s over-leveraged investment houses began to fail in September 2008, the leaders of the Republican and Democratic Parties, heads of major corporations, and opinion leaders stretching from the *National Review* and the *Wall Street Journal* on the right to *The Nation* on the left, agreed that spending some $700 billion to buy the investors' "toxic assets" was the only alternative to the U.S. economy's "systemic collapse." In this, President George W. Bush and his would-be Republican successor John McCain agreed with the Democratic candidate, Barack Obama. Many, if not most, people around them also agreed upon the eventual commitment of some ten trillion non-existent dollars in ways unprecedented in America. They explained neither the difference between the assets' nominal and real values, nor precisely why letting the market find the latter would collapse America's economy. In part because they deem the American people incapable of understanding such matters, in part because they do not understand them themselves, they failed to think these matters through for themselves. When dealing with the American people, as when dealing with children and animals, they promised rewards if their policies were implemented, and threatened doom if they were not. The public objected immediately, by margins of three or four to one. A January 2009 CNN poll found that 80 percent opposed the proposed measures.

When this majority discovered that virtually no one with a national voice or in a position of power in either party would take their objections seriously, that decisions about their money were being made in bipartisan backroom deals with interested parties, and that the laws on these matters were being voted on by people who had not read them, they realized that America's rulers had become a self-contained, self-referential class. Then, after those in power changed their plans from buying toxic assets to buying up equity in banks and major industries but refused to explain why, when they reasserted their right to decide ad hoc on these and so many other matters, supposing them to be beyond the general public's understanding, the American people started referring to those in and around the government as the Ruling Class.

While Europeans are accustomed to being ruled by presumed betters whom they distrust, the American people's realization of being ruled in the same way shocked this country into well-nigh revolutionary attitudes. But only the realization was new. The Ruling Class had sunk deep roots in America decades before 2008. Machiavelli compares serious political diseases to the Aetolian fevers—easy to treat early on when they are difficult to discern, but virtually untreatable by the time they become obvious.

America's disease is all the more deadly for being bipartisan. Republican and Democratic office-holders and their retinues share a similar presumption to dominate, and show fewer differences in tastes, habits, opinions, and sources of income among one another than between both and the rest of the country. They think, look, and act as a class, almost a caste.

Although after the election of 2008, most Republican office holders argued against the Troubled Asset Relief Program, against the subsequent bailouts of the auto industry, against the several "stimulus" bills and further summary expansions of government power to benefit clients of government at the expense of ordinary citizens, the American people had every reason to believe that many Republican politicians were doing so simply by the logic of partisan opposition. After all, Republicans had been happy enough to approve of similar things under Republican administrations. Differences between Bushes, Clintons, and Obamas are of degree, not kind. Moreover, the 2009–10 establishment Republicans sought only to modify the government's agenda, while showing eagerness to join the Democrats in new grand schemes, if only they were allowed to. Senator Orrin Hatch continued to dream of being Ted Kennedy, while Lindsey Graham set aside what is true or false about "global warming" for the sake of getting on what he imagined to be "the right side of history." No prominent Republican challenged the Ruling Class' continued claim of superior insight, nor its denigration of the American people as irritable children who must learn their place. The Republican Party did not disparage the Ruling Class, because most of its officials are or would like to be part of it.

The polls quantify what any observant person can see: the division between the Ruling Class and the Country Class has overwhelmed that between Republicans and Democrats. When pollsters ask the American people whether they are likely to vote Republican or Democrat in the next presidential election, Republicans win growing pluralities. But whenever pollsters add the preferences "undecided," "none of the above," or "Tea Party," these win handily, the Democrats come in second, and the Republicans trail far behind. That's because while most of the voters who call themselves Democrats say that Democratic officials represent them well, only a fourth of the voters who identify themselves as Republicans say the same about the Republican officeholders. Hence our rulers, both Democrats and Republicans, gladden the hearts of some one-third of the electorate—most Democratic voters, plus a few Republicans. This means that Democratic politicians are the Ruling Class' prime legitimate representatives, and that because Republican politicians are supported by only a fourth of their voters while the rest vote for them reluctantly, most are aspirants for a junior role in the

Ruling Class. In short, the Ruling Class has a party: the Democrats. But some two-thirds of Americans—a few Democratic voters, most Republican voters, and all Independents—lack a vehicle in electoral politics.

Sooner or later, well or badly, that majority's demand for representation will be filled. Whereas in 1968 Governor George Wallace's taunt that "there ain't a dime's worth of difference" between the Republican and Democratic Parties resonated with only 13.5 percent of the American people, in 1992 Ross Perot became a serious contender for the presidency (at one point he was favored by 39 percent of Americans, vs. 31 percent for George H. W. Bush and 25 percent for Clinton) simply by speaking ill of the Ruling Class. Today, few speak well of the Ruling Class. Not only has it burgeoned in size and pretense, but it also has undertaken wars it has not won, presided over a declining economy and a ballooning debt, made life more expensive, raised taxes, and talked down to the American people. Hence, in recent years, Americans' conviction that the Ruling Class is as hostile as it is incompetent has solidified. The polls tell us that only about a fifth of Americans trust the government to do the right thing. The rest expect that it will do more harm than good and are no longer afraid to say so.

The two classes have less in common culturally,

dislike each other more, and embody ways of life more different from one another than did the nineteenth century's Northerners and Southerners—nearly all of whom, as Lincoln reminded them, "prayed to the same God." By contrast, while most Americans pray to the God "who hath created and doth sustain us," our Ruling Class prays to itself as saviors of the planet and improvers of humanity. Our classes' clash is over whose country America is, over what way of life will prevail, over who is to defer to whom about what. The gravity of such divisions points us, as it did Lincoln, to Mark's Gospel: "If a house be divided against itself, that house cannot stand."

Far from speculating about how the political confrontation might develop between America's Ruling Class—relatively few people supported by no more than one-third of Americans—and a Country Party comprising two-thirds of the populace, our task here is to understand the divisions that underlie that confrontation's unpredictable future.

CHAPTER 2

The Ruling Class

"We are governed at all levels by America's luckiest children, sons and daughters of the abundance, and they call themselves optimists but they're not optimists—they're unimaginative."

—PEGGY NOONAN,
The Wall Street Journal, November 5, 2009

Who are these rulers, and by what right do they rule? How did America change from a place where people could expect to live without bowing to privileged classes to one in which, at best, they might have the chance to climb into them? What sets our Ruling Class apart from the rest of us?

Never has there been so little diversity within America's upper crust. Always, in America as elsewhere, some people have been wealthier and more powerful than others. But until our own time, America's upper crust was a mixture of people who had gained prominence in a variety of ways, who drew their money and status from different sources, and who were not predictably of one mind on any given matter. The Boston Brahmins; the New York financiers; the land barons of California, Texas, and Florida; the industrialists of Pittsburgh; the Southern aristocracy; and the hardscrabble politicians who made it big in Chicago or Memphis had little contact with one another. Few had much contact with government, and "bureaucrat" was a dirty word for all. So was "social engineering." Nor had the schools and universities that formed yesterday's upper crust imposed a single orthodoxy about the origins of man, about American history, or about how America should be governed. All that has changed.

Today's Ruling Class, from Boston to San Diego, was formed by an educational system that exposed them to the same ideas and gave them remarkably uniform guidance, as well as tastes and habits. These amount to a social canon of judgments about good and evil, complete with secular sacred history, sins (against minorities and the environment), and saints. Using the right words and avoiding the wrong ones when referring to such matters—speaking the "in" language—serves as a badge of identity. Regardless of what business or profession they are in, their road up included government channels and government money, because as government has grown, the boundary between it and the rest of American life has become indistinct. Many in the Ruling Class began their careers in government and leveraged their way into the private sector. Some (e.g., Secretary of the Treasury Timothy Geithner) have never held a non-government job. Hence, whether formally in government, out of it, or halfway in, America's Ruling Class speaks the language and has the tastes, habits, and tools of bureaucrats. It rules uneasily over the majority of Americans who are not oriented to government.

Why has this happened? The most widespread answers—by people such as the *New York Times*' Thomas Friedman and David Brooks—are schlock sociology. Supposedly, modern society became so complex and productive, and the technical skills to run it so rare, that it called forth a new class of highly educated officials and cooperators in an ever less private sector. Similarly fanciful is Edward Goldberg's notion that America is now ruled by a "newocracy": a "new aristocracy who are the true beneficiaries of globalization—including the multinational manager, the technologist, and the aspirational members of the meritocracy." In fact, our Ruling Class grew and set itself apart from the rest of us by its connection with ever bigger government, and above all by a certain attitude.

Other explanations are counterintuitive. Wealth? The heads of the class do live in our big cities' priciest enclaves and suburbs, from Montgomery County, Maryland; to Palo Alto, California; to Boston's Beacon Hill, as well as in opulent university towns from Princeton to Boulder. But they are no wealthier than many Texas oilmen or California farmers, or their neighbors with whom they do not associate—just as the social science and humanities class that rules universities seldom associates with physicians and physicists. Rather, regardless of where they live, the Ruling Class' social and intellectual circle includes people in the lucrative "nonprofit" and "philanthropic" sectors and in public policy.

What really distinguishes these privileged people demographically is that, whether in government power directly or as officers in companies, their careers and fortunes depend on government. They vote Democrat more consistently than those who live on any of America's Dr. Martin Luther King, Jr. streets. These socioeconomic opposites draw their money and orientation from the same sources as the millions of teachers, consultants, and government employees in the middle ranks who aspire to be the former and identify morally with what they suppose to be the latter's grievances.

Professional prominence or position will not secure a place in the Ruling Class any more than mere money. In fact, it is possible to be an official of a major corporation or a member of the U.S. Supreme Court (just ask Justice Clarence Thomas), or even president of the nation (Ronald Reagan), and not be taken seriously by the Ruling Class. Like a fraternity, this class requires, above all, comity—being in with the right people, giving the required signs that one is on the right side, and joining in despising the Outs. Once an official or professional shows that he shares the manners, the tastes, and the interests of the class, gives lip service to its ideals and shibboleths, and is willing to accommodate the interests of its senior members, he gains the presumption of competence as well as access to the establishment's countless profitable connections. Republicans salivate for that status.

If, for example, you were Laurence Tribe in 1984, Harvard professor of law and leftist pillar of the establishment, you could "write" your magnum opus by using the work of your student assistants, including Ron Klain. A decade later, after Klain admitted to having written some parts of the book, and other parts were found to be verbatim or paraphrases of a book published in 1974, you could claim (perhaps correctly) that your plagiarism was "inadvertent," and you could count on the law school's dean, Elena Kagan, to appoint a committee (including former and future Harvard President

Derek Bok) that would issue a secret report that "closed" the incident. (Incidentally, Kagan ended up a justice of the Supreme Court.) Not one of these people did their jobs—the professor did not write the book himself, the professor or some assistant plagiarized instead of researching, the dean and the committee did not hold the professor accountable—and yet all ended up rewarded.

To corruption, the Ruling Class adds hypocrisy: for example, if non–Ruling Class people write learned papers and lead distinguished careers in climatology at, say, MIT (Richard Lindzen) or UVA (S. Fred Singer), this is not enough for their questions about "global warming" to be taken seriously. For our Ruling Class, identity always trumps truth.

Much less does membership in the Ruling Class depend on high academic achievement. To see something closer to an academic meritocracy, consider France, where elected officials have little power, a vast bureaucracy explicitly controls the minutest details of everyday life, from how babies are raised to how to make cheese, and people get into and advance within that bureaucracy strictly on the basis of competitive exams. Hence, for good or ill, France's Ruling Class is made up of bright people—certifiably. Not ours. But didn't ours go to Harvard and Princeton and Stanford? Didn't most of them get good grades? Yes. But while getting into the École Nationale d'Administration or the École Polytechnique or the dozens of other entry points to France's Ruling Class requires outperforming others in blindly graded exams, and graduating from such places requires passing exams that many fail, getting into America's "top" schools is less a matter of passing exams than of showing up with acceptable grades (American secondary schools are generous with their As) and a social profile that fits the school's image of itself. America's top-tier schools advertise that they lower their standards for "minorities" (not including Asians). Moreover, the whites they admit are not necessarily the ones with the best SAT scores. Rather, they tend to be children of members of the upper-middle class or aspirants of the Ruling Class. Few whites from humble backgrounds, never mind Christians, are to be found. The top schools select for compatibility, not excellence.

Moreover, it is an open secret that the "best" colleges require the least work and give out the highest grade-point averages. These schools have been the national leaders in grade inflation. At Stanford, where the most common grade is an A, a student complained to the *Daily* that his classes' academic content got in the way of the reason he had chosen the school—learning how to run the country.

No, our Ruling Class recruits and renews itself not through meritocracy but rather by taking into itself people whose most prominent feature is their commitment to fit in. The most successful neither write books and papers that stand up to criticism nor release their academic records. It is reasonable to ask of those who accuse others of being dumb, "What are his test scores?" But the Ruling Class won't answer. Thus does our Ruling Class stunt itself through negative selection. Each succeeding generation is less competent than its predecessor. But the more it has dumbed itself down, the more it has defined itself by the presumption of intellectual superiority. In this way, too, it has discredited itself.

The Key to Arrogance

This presumption is key to understanding our bipartisan Ruling Class. Its first tenet is that its members are the best and brightest, while the rest of Americans are retrograde, racist, and dysfunctional unless properly constrained. How did this replace the Founding Fathers' paradigm that "all men are created equal"?

The notion of human equality was always a hard sell, because experience teaches us that we are so unequal in so many ways, and because making oneself superior is so tempting that Lincoln called it "the old serpent: you work, I'll eat." But human equality made sense to our Founding Fathers, because they believed that all men are made in the image and likeness of God, because they were yearning for equal treatment under British law, or because they had read John Locke.

It did not take long for their paradigm to be challenged by interest and by "science." By the 1820s, as J. C. Calhoun was reading in the best London journals that different breeds of animals and plants produce inferior or superior results, slave owners were citing the Negroes' deficiencies in order to argue that they should remain slaves indefinitely. Lots of others were reading Ludwig Feuerbach's rendition of Hegelian philosophy, according to which biblical injunctions reflect alienated human beings' best fantasies, or, in the young Karl Marx's formulation, that ethical thought is "superstructural" to material reality. By 1853, when Senator John Pettit of Ohio called "all men are created equal" "a self-evident lie," much of America's educated class had already absorbed the "scientific" notion (which Darwin only popularized) that man is the product of chance mutation and natural selection of the fittest. Accordingly, by nature, superior men subdue inferior ones just as they subdue lower beings, or try to improve them as they please. Hence, while it pleased the abolitionists to believe in freeing Negroes and improving them, it also pleased them to believe that Southerners had to be punished and reconstructed by force. In short, Darwinism corrupted Northern and Southern thinkers equally. As the nineteenth century ended, the educated class' religious fervor turned to social reform: they were sure that because man is a mere part of evolutionary nature, man could be improved, and that they, the most highly evolved of all, were the improvers.

Thus began the Progressive Era. When Woodrow Wilson in 1914 was asked, "Can't you let anything alone?" he answered with, "I let everything alone that you can show me is not itself moving in the wrong direction, but I am not going to let those things alone that I see are going downhill." Wilson spoke for the thousands of well-off Americans who patronized the spas at places like Chautauqua and Lake Mohonk. By such upper-middle-class waters, progressives who imagined themselves to be the world's examples and the world's reformers dreamed big dreams of establishing order, justice, and peace at home and abroad. Neither were they shy about their desire for power. Wilson was the first American statesman to argue that the Founders had done badly by depriving the

U.S. government of the power to reshape American society. Nor was Wilson the last to invade a foreign country (Mexico) to "teach [them] to elect good men."

World War I and the chaos at home and abroad that followed it discredited the progressives in the American people's eyes. Their international schemes had brought blood and promised more. Their domestic management had not improved Americans' lives, but had instead given them a taste of arbitrary government, including Prohibition. The progressives, for their part, found it fulfilling to attribute their schemes' failure to the American people's backwardness, to something deeply wrong with America. The American people had failed because democracy in its American form perpetuated the worst in humanity. Thus progressives began to look down on the masses, to look on themselves as the vanguard, and to look abroad for examples to emulate.

The cultural divide between the "educated class" and the rest of the country opened in the interwar years. Some progressives joined the "vanguard of the proletariat," the Communist Party. Many more were deeply sympathetic to Soviet Russia, as they were to Fascist Italy and Nazi Germany. Not just *The Nation*, but also the *New York Times* and *National Geographic* found much to be imitated in these regimes, because they promised energetically to transcend their peoples' ways and to build "the new man." Above all, our educated class was bitter about America. In 1925, the American Civil Liberties Union sponsored a legal challenge to a Tennessee law that required teaching the biblical account of creation. The ensuing trial, broadcast nationally on the radio, as well as the subsequent hit movie *Inherit the Wind*, were the occasion for what one might have called the Chautauqua Class to drive home the point that Americans who believed in the Bible were willful ignoramuses. Clarence Darrow ridiculed the notion that any rights derive from nature because it is ever-evolving, much less from God.

As World War II approached, some American progressives supported the Soviet Union (and its ally, Nazi Germany), and others Great Britain and France. But progressives agreed on one thing: the approaching war should be blamed on the majority of Americans, because they had refused to lead the League of Nations. Darryl Zanuck produced the critically acclaimed movie [Woodrow] *Wilson*, featuring Cedric Hardwicke as the villainous Senator Henry Cabot Lodge, who, by appealing to American narrow-mindedness against Wilson's benevolent genius, kept America out of the League of Nations and thus allegedly brought on the war.

Franklin Roosevelt began the process that turned the

Chautauqua Class into rulers by bringing them into his administration. FDR described America's problems in technocratic terms. America's problems would be fixed by a "brain trust." Power would define who was brainy and who was not. His New Deal's solutions—the administrative state, made up of the alphabet-soup of "independent" agencies that have run America ever since—turned many progressives into powerful bureaucrats, and then into lobbyists. As the saying goes, they came to Washington to do good, and stayed to do well.

As their number and sense of importance grew, so did their distaste for common Americans. This progressive class, believing itself "scientific," sought to explain its differences from and authority over its neighbors in "scientific" terms. The most elaborate of these attempts was Theodor Adorno's widely acclaimed *The Authoritarian Personality* (1948). It invented a set of criteria by which to define personality traits, ranked these traits and their intensity in any given person on what it called the "F scale" (F for fascist), interviewed hundreds of Americans, and concluded that most who were not liberal Democrats were latent fascists. This way of thinking about non-progressives filtered down to college curricula. In 1963–64, for example, I was assigned Herbert McCloskey's *Conservatism and Personality* (1958) at Rutgers' Eagleton Institute of

Politics as a paradigm of methodological correctness. The author had defined conservatism in terms of answers to certain questions, defined a number of personality disorders in terms of other questions, and run a survey that proved "scientifically" that conservatives were maladjusted, ne'er-do-well ignoramuses. (My class project, titled "Liberalism and Personality," following the same methodology, proved just as "scientifically" that liberals suffered from the very same social diseases, along with even more amusing ones.)

The point is this: though not one in a thousand members of today's bipartisan Ruling Class have ever heard of Adorno or McCloskey, much less can explain the Feuerbachian-Marxist notion that human judgments are "epiphenomenal" products of spiritual or material alienation, the notion that the common people's words are, like grunts, mere signs of pain, pleasure, and frustration, is now axiomatic among our Ruling Class. They absorbed it osmotically, second- or third-hand, from their education and from their companions. Truly, after Barack Obama described his opponents' clinging to "God and guns" as a characteristic of inferior Americans, he justified himself by pointing out he had said "what *everybody* knows is true."

Confident "knowledge" that "some of us, the ones who matter," have grasped truths that the common herd cannot, truths that direct us, truths the comprehension of which entitles us to discount what the ruled say and to presume what they mean, made our progressives into a class long before they took power. It cannot be emphasized enough that this is not an opinion, a mere point of view that the Ruling Class' members may abandon in the face of massive evidence to the contrary. Rather, the sense of intellectual and social superiority over the common herd is arguably the main component of millions of people's self-conception. Such people can no more believe that a Christian might be their intellectual and moral equal than white Southerners of the Jim Crow era could think the same of Negroes.

Meddling and Apologies

America's best and brightest believe themselves qualified and duty-bound to direct the lives not only of Americans, but of foreigners as well. George W. Bush's 2005 inaugural statement that America cannot be free until the whole world is free, and hence that America must push and prod mankind to freedom, was but an extrapolation of the sentiments of America's progressive class, first articulated by people such as Princeton's Woodrow Wilson and Columbia's Nicholas Murray

Butler. But while the early progressives expected the rest of the world to follow peacefully, today's Ruling Class makes decisions about war and peace at least as much to forcibly tinker with the innards of foreign bodies politic as to protect America. Indeed, they conflate the two purposes. By contrast, the American people draw a bright line between war against our enemies and peace with non-enemies in whose affairs we do not interfere. That's why, from Wilson to Kissinger, the Ruling Class has complained that the American people oscillate between bellicosity and isolationism.

Because our Ruling Class deems unsophisticated the American people's perennial preference for decisive military action or none, its default solution to international threats has been to commit blood and treasure to long-term, twilight efforts to reform the world's Vietnams, Somalias, Iraqs, and Afghanistans, believing that changing hearts and minds is the prerequisite of peace, and that it knows how to change them. The apparently endless series of wars in which our Ruling Class has embroiled America, wars that have achieved nothing worthwhile at great cost in lives and treasure, has contributed to defining it, and to discrediting it—but not in its own eyes.

Rather, even as our Ruling Class has lectured, cajoled, and sometimes intruded violently to reform foreign countries in its own image, it has apologized to them for America not having matched that image—their private image. Woodrow Wilson began this double game in 1919, when he assured Europe's peoples that America had mandated him to demand their agreement to Article X of the peace treaty (the League of Nations), and then swore to the American people that Article X was the Europeans' non-negotiable demand. The fact that the U.S. government had seized control of transatlantic cable communications helped to hide (for a while) that the League scheme was merely the American progressives' private dream. In our time, this double game is quotidian on the evening news.

Notably, President Obama apologized to Europe because "the United States has fallen short of meeting its responsibilities" to reduce carbon emissions by taxation. But the American people never assumed such responsibility, and continue to oppose doing so. Hence, President Obama was not apologizing for anything that he or anyone he respected had done, but rather blaming his fellow Americans for not doing what he thinks they should do, all while glossing over the fact that the Europeans had done the taxing but not the reducing. Wilson redux.

Similarly, Obama "apologized" to Europeans because some Americans—not him and his friends, naturally—had shown "arrogance and been dismissive" toward them, and to the world, because President Truman had used the atom bomb to end World War II. So President Clinton apologized to Africans because some Americans held African slaves until 1865 and others were mean to Negroes thereafter— not himself and his friends, of course. So Assistant Secretary of State Michael Posner apologized to Chinese diplomats for Arizona's law that directs police to check immigration status.

Republicans engage in that sort of thing as well: former Soviet dictator Mikhail Gorbachev has said that in 1987, then–Vice President George H. W. Bush distanced himself from his own administration by telling Gorbachev, "Reagan is a conservative, an extreme conservative. All the dummies and blockheads are with him." This is all about a class of Americans distinguishing itself from its inferiors. It recalls the Pharisee in the Temple: "Lord, I thank thee that I am not like other men."

In sum, our Ruling Class does not like the rest of America. Most of all, it dislikes that so many Americans think America is substantially different from the rest of the world—and like it that way. For our Ruling Class, however, America is a work in progress, just like the rest the world, and they are the engineers.

CHAPTER 3

Power and Privilege

"Commerce is the profession of equals."
—MONTESQIEU, *The Spirit of the Laws*

"The question is," said Alice, "whether you can make words mean so many different things."
—LEWIS CARROLL, *Alice in Wonderland*

"We will restore science to its rightful place."
—BARACK OBAMA, 2009 inaugural speech

Power

Our Ruling Class' agenda is power for itself. It seeks and exercises that power through unremarkable patronage and promises thereof, as well as by courting supporters and denigrating opponents. These ordinary means, however, are having remarkable effects on America's body politic, because their practice is wrapped up in our Ruling Class' peculiar intellectual and moral pretenses. Chief among these is its ideological belief that it has an exclusive, Gnostic grip on modern science's secrets. Nevertheless, as we look at how our Ruling Class is making our economic livelihood ever more dependent on itself, at how it is running a system of representation and a legal system quite opposite to those bequeathed to us by our founders, as well as at how it is disaggregating our families and dispiriting our souls, let us keep in mind that this agenda is driven primarily by mundane personal interest. This agenda proceeds from claims that our Ruling Class knows formulae for spreading economic wealth, for engineering social happiness, and for legal and constitutional fairness. It claims as well to be more resistant than the rest of us to the temptation to profit personally from power. In short, it proceeds from the premise of human inequality and leads to even greater inequality. But, pretenses notwithstanding, our Ruling Class was no more present at the creation of our nation than the rest of us, nor are they any less self interested. Its members too put on their pants one leg at a time.

Our Ruling Class is a machine. That is, it lives by providing tangible rewards to its members. "Machine parties" around the world often provide rank-and-file activists with modest livelihoods, and enhance mightily the upper level members' wealth. Because of this, whatever else such parties might accomplish, they must feed the machine by transferring money or jobs or privileges—civic as well as economic—to the party's clients, whether directly or indirectly. This, incidentally, is close to Aristotle's view of democracy.

Hence, our Ruling Class' first priority in any and all matters, its solution to any and all problems, is to increase the power of the government—meaning of those who run it, meaning themselves. Secondly it is to recompense political supporters with public money, privileged jobs, contracts, etc. That is why our Ruling Class' solution, not just for economic downturns and social ills but also for hurricanes and tornadoes, global cooling and global warming, has been to claim more power for itself. A priori, one might wonder whether enriching and empowering individuals of a certain kind can make Americans kinder and gentler, much less control the weather. *But there can be no doubt that such power and money makes Americans ever more dependent on those who wield it.* Let us now look at what this means in our time.

Dependence Economics

By taxing and parceling out more than a third of what Americans produce, through regulations that reach deep into American life, our Ruling Class is making itself the arbiter of wealth and poverty. While the economic value of anything depends on sellers and buyers agreeing on that value as civil equals in the absence of force, modern government is about nothing if not tampering with civil equality. By endowing some in society with the power to force others to sell cheaper than they would like to, and forcing others yet to buy at higher prices—or even to buy in the first place—modern government makes valuable some things that are not, and devalues others that are. Whatever else government may be, it is inherently a factory of privilege and inequality. Thus, if you are not among the favored guests at the table where officials make detailed lists of who is to receive what at whose expense, you are on the menu. Eventually, pretending forcibly that valueless things have value dilutes the currency's value for all. But that matters not at all to those at the table.

Laws and regulations nowadays are longer than ever, because length is needed to specify how people will be treated unequally. For example, the healthcare bill of 2010 takes more than 2,700 pages to make sure not just that some states will be treated differently from others because their senators offered key political support, but more importantly to codify bargains between the government and various parts of the healthcare industry, state governments, and large employers regarding who would receive what benefits (e.g., public employee unions and auto workers) and who would pass what indirect taxes on to the general public. The financial regulation bill of 2010, far from setting unequivocal rules for the entire financial industry in few words, spends some 2,500 pages tilting the field toward some and away from others. After the bill's passage, the *New York Times* reported that the financial industry's larger firms were hiring highly paid former federal regulators to conduct the negotiations that would spell out the law's real meaning for each of them.

Even more significantly, these and other products of Democratic and Republican administrations and Congresses empower countless boards and commissions to arbitrarily protect some persons and companies while ruining others. These laws' real meaning emerges from the charters that these boards and commissions write for themselves, from the identities of

the persons appointed to run them, and from the policies on which they settle. Thus, in 2008, the Republican administration first bailed out Bear Stearns, then
let Lehman Brothers sink in the ensuing panic, but
then rescued Goldman Sachs by infusing cash into its
principal debtor, AIG. Then its Democratic successor
used similarly naked discretionary power (and money
appropriated for another purpose) to give major stakes
in the auto industry to labor unions that support it.
Nowadays, the members of our Ruling Class admit
that they do not read the laws. They don't have to!
Because modern laws are primarily grants of discretion, all anybody has to know about them is whom
they empower.

This defines "crony capitalism." The regulators
and the regulated become indistinguishable, and
they prosper together because they have the power
to restrict the public's choices in ways that channel
money to themselves and their political supporters.
Most of the world is too well acquainted with this
way of economic life. Americans are just starting to
find out. By making economic rules dependent on
discretion, our bipartisan Ruling Class teaches that
prosperity is to be bought with the coin of political
support. Thus in the 1990s and 2000s, as Democrats
and Republicans forced banks to make loans for houses

to people and at rates they would not otherwise have considered, builders and investors had every reason to make as much money as they could from the ensuing inflation of housing prices. When the bubble burst, only those connected with the Ruling Class, at the bottom and the top, were bailed out—at the expense of the "unconnected majority."

Similarly, by taxing the use of carbon fuels and subsidizing "alternative energy," our Ruling Class created arguably the world's biggest opportunity for making money out of things that few, if any, would buy absent its intervention. The prospect of legislation that would put a price on carbon emissions and allot certain amounts to certain companies set off a feeding frenzy among large companies to show support for a "green agenda," because such allotments would be worth some $1.2 *trillion* in the first ten years. All of those dollars would come from higher energy prices imposed on consumers. That is why companies hired some 2,500 lobbyists in 2009 to deepen their involvement in "climate change." At the very least, such involvement benefits them by making them into privileged collectors of carbon taxes. The revenue would finance "green" contracts and subcontracts, jobs and consultancies galore, paying millions of Americans to produce otherwise unsalable goods, and living in privileged lifestyles at the expense of their less well connected neighbors. For example, the ethanol industry exists exclusively because legislation mandates the use of its subsidized product. The U.S. government pays producers $1.78 per gallon in direct subsidies and tariffs. After Americans pay for ethanol through taxes, they get to pay higher prices at the pump—another massive diversion of wealth from ordinary people who are forced to buy an inferior product at a higher price, to the privileged people who set the rules. What effect creating such privileges may have on "global warming" is debatable. But such privileges surely increase the number of people dependent on the Ruling Class, and teach Americans that satisfying that class is a surer way of making a living than producing goods and services that people want to buy.

Beyond patronage, picking economic winners and losers redirects the American people's energies to tasks that the political class deems more worthy than what Americans choose for themselves. John Kenneth Galbraith's characterization of America's economy as "private wealth amidst public squalor" (*The Affluent Society*, 1958) encapsulates the complaint of our best and brightest: left to themselves, Americans use land inefficiently in suburbs and exurbs, making it necessary to use energy to transport them to jobs and shopping. Americans drive big cars, eat lots of meat and other unhealthy things, and go to the doctor whenever they feel like it. Americans think it is just to spend the money they earn to satisfy their private desires, even though the Ruling Class knows that justice lies in improving the community and the planet. The Ruling Class knows that Americans must learn to live more densely and closer to work, that they must drive smaller cars, if they drive at all, that they must change their lives to use less energy, that their dietary habits must improve, that they must accept limits on how much medical care they get, that they must divert more of their money to support those people, cultural enterprises, and plans for the planet that the Ruling Class deems worthy. So ever-greater taxes and intrusive regulations are the main wrenches by which the American people can be improved (and, yes, by which the Ruling Class exercises its privileges and grows).

The 2010 medical law is a template for the Ruling Class' economic modus operandi: the government taxes citizens to pay for medical care and requires citizens to purchase health insurance. The money thus taken and directed is money that the citizens themselves might have used to pay for medical care.

In exchange for the money, the government promises that care will be available through its system. But then all the boards, commissions, guidelines, procedures, and "best practices" that constitute the system become the arbiters of what any citizen ends up getting. The citizen might end up dissatisfied with what the system offers. But when he gave up his money, he gave up the power to choose, and became dependent on all the boards and commissions that his money also pays for and that raise the cost of care.

Similarly, in 2008, the House Ways and Means Committee began considering a plan to force citizens who own Individual Retirement Accounts (IRAs) to transfer those funds into government-run "guaranteed retirement accounts." If the government can force citizens to trade private access to medical care for government-guaranteed health insurance, by what logic can it *not* force us to trade private ownership and control of private retirement accounts for government-guaranteed retirement accounts? If our body politic credits the Ruling Class' claim that it has the right and the expertise to preempt individuals' decisions on the use of money for healthcare, how can it not credit its claim to rightly preempt individuals' decisions about where to put their retirement nest egg?

In sum, our Ruling Class' economics aim not at

making us wealthier, but at making us more dependent. Thus does it deny the principle of human equality.

Who Depends on Whom?

In *Congressional Government* (1885), Woodrow Wilson left no doubt: the U.S. Constitution prevents the government from meeting the country's needs by enumerating rights on which the government may not infringe. ("Congress shall make no law . . . " says the First Amendment, typically.) But Wilson bemoaned the fact that the Constitution does not permit government to deal adequately with "modern industrial organization, including banks, corporations, joint-stock companies, financial devices, national debts, paper currency, national systems of taxation . . . so that the play of the civil institutions shall not alter the play of the economic forces, [and thus accurately regulate] the complication and delicacy of the industrial system." Wilson wrote that competent government must be like "a foreman [who] take[s] a hand in the work which he guides; and so I suppose our legislation must be likened to a poor foreman, because it stands altogether apart from that work which it is set to see well done." A competent government must also have full power "to remedy the mistakes of the legislation of the past." So Wilson, and the class in which he was so prominent, simply "pushed the envelope" of constitutional limits, especially during "crises," slowly, practically, to craft a "living" Constitution that does not so much restrict government as it confers "positive rights"—meaning charters of government power. Thus they slowly buried eighteenth-century words with twentieth-century practice.

Wilson thought our electoral system was as much a barrier to progress as is the Constitution. That is because our system, based on single-member districts, empowers individual voters at the expense of "responsible parties." For Wilson, the connection between voters and elected officials was problematic. Wilson wanted voters to choose between two parties, with the winner having broad powers to run the country. Following Wilson, American progressives have always wanted to turn the U.S. Congress from the role defined by James Madison's *Federalist #10*—"refine and enlarge the public's view"—to something like the British Parliament, which ratifies government actions. Although Britain's electoral system—like ours, single members elected in historic districts by plurality vote—had made members of Parliament (MPs) responsive to their constituents in ancient times, by Wilson's time the growing importance of parties made MPs beholden to party leaders. Hence, whoever controls the majority party controls both Parliament and the government. That's why the Ruling Class' perpetual agenda has been to diminish the role of the citizenry's elected representatives, enhancing that of party leaders—a class apart from the voters.

In America, the process by which party has become (almost) as important began with the Supreme Court's 1962 decision in *Baker v. Carr*, which, by setting the single standard of "one man, one vote" for congressional districts, ended up legitimizing the practice of gerrymandering, or concentrating the opposition party's voters into as few districts as possible while placing one's own voters into as many as possible in an attempt to yield victories. Republican and Democratic state legislatures have gerrymandered for half a century. That's why today's Congress consists more and more of persons who represent their respective party establishments—not nearly as much as in Britain, but it is heading in that direction. Once districts are gerrymandered "safe" for one party or another, the voters therein count less, because party leaders can count more on elected legislators to toe the party line.

To the extent that party leaders do not have to worry about voters, they can choose privileged interlocutors, representing those in society whom they find most amenable. In America, ever more since the 1930s—elsewhere in the world this practice is ubiquitous and long-standing—government has designated certain individuals, companies, and organizations within each of society's sectors as (junior) partners in elaborating laws and administrative rules for those sectors. The government empowers the persons it has chosen over those not chosen, deems them the sector's true representatives, and rewards them. They become part of the Ruling Class.

Thus in 2009–10, the American Medical Association (AMA) strongly supported the new medical care law, which the administration touted as having the support of "the doctors," even though the vast majority of America's 975,000 physicians opposed it. Those who run the AMA, however, have a government contract as exclusive providers of the codes by which physicians and hospitals bill the government for their services. The millions of dollars that flow thereby to the AMA's officers keep them in line, while the impracticality of doing without the billing codes tamps down rebellion in the doctors' ranks. When the administration wanted to bolster its case that the state of Arizona's enforcement of federal immigration laws was offensive to Hispanics, the National Association of Chiefs of Police—whose officials depend on the administration for their salaries—issued a statement claiming that the laws would endanger all Americans by raising Hispanics' animosity. This reflected conversations with the administration rather than a vote of the nation's police chiefs.

Similarly, modern labor unions are no longer bunches of workers banding together, and are instead groups of persons bundled under the aegis of an organization chosen jointly by employers and government. The U.S. labor movement now consists almost exclusively of government employees, employees of companies doing government contracts, or companies that are subsidized by government. Like their counterparts around the world, they trade political contributions and votes for guaranteed contracts. Prototypical is the Service Employees International Union (SEIU), which grew spectacularly by persuading managers of government agencies as well as of publicly funded private entities that placing their employees in the SEIU would relieve them of responsibility. Not by being elected by workers' secret ballots did the SEIU conquer workplace after workplace, but rather by such deals, or by the union presenting what it claimed were cards from workers who approved of the representation. The union gets 2 percent of the workers' pay, which it recycles as contributions to the Democratic Party, which is then translated into greater power over public employees. The union's leadership is part of the Ruling Class' beating heart.

The point is that a doctor, a building contractor, a janitor, or a schoolteacher only counts in today's America insofar as he is part of the hierarchy of a sector organization affiliated with the Ruling Class. Less and less do such persons count as voters.

Ordinary people have also gone a long way toward losing equal treatment under the law. The America described in civics books—in which no one could be convicted or fined except by a jury of his peers for having violated laws passed by elected representatives—started disappearing when the New Deal inaugurated today's administrative state, in which bureaucrats make, enforce, and adjudicate nearly all the rules. Today's legal and administrative texts are incomprehensibly detailed and freighted with provisions crafted specifically to affect equal individuals unequally. The bureaucrats do not enforce the rules themselves so much as whatever "agency policy" they choose to draw from them in any given case. If you protest any "agency policy," you will be informed that it was formulated with input from "the public"—but not from the likes of you.

Disregard for the text of laws, for the dictionary definition of words and the intentions of those who wrote them, in favor of the decider's discretion has permeated our Ruling Class from the Supreme Court to the lowest local agency. Ever since Oliver Wendell Holmes argued in 1920 (*Missouri v. Holland*) that presidents, Congresses, and judges could not be bound by the U.S. Constitution regarding matters that the people who wrote and ratified it could not have foreseen, it has become conventional wisdom among our Ruling Class that they may transcend the Constitution while pretending allegiance to it. They began by stretching such constitutional terms as "interstate commerce" and "due process," then transmuting others, e.g., "search and seizure," into "privacy." Thus in 1973, the Supreme Court endowed its invention of "privacy" with a "penumbra" that it deemed "broad enough to encompass a woman's decision whether or not to terminate her pregnancy." *The court gave no other constitutional reasoning, period.* Perfunctory to the point of mockery, this constitutional talk was to reassure the American people that the Ruling Class was acting within the Constitution's limitations. By the 1990s, federal courts were invalidating amendments to state constitutions passed by referenda to secure the "positive rights" they invent, because these expressions of popular will were inconsistent with the Constitution they themselves were construing.

In 2010 a Federal Judge declared "unconstitutional" the people of California's referendum approval of a state constitutional amendment defining marriage as between one man and one woman. Consider: with which constitution was the people of California's action inconsistent? Certainly not with the US Constitution, ratified by the American people in 1787, or with any amendment thereto. That Constitution does not mention marriage, any more than abortion. Moreover, any reference to what those who wrote and ratified that Constitution had in mind when they thought of marriage or abortion lends no support whatever to the notion that restricting marriage to one man and one woman was repugnant to them any more than restricting abortion was.

So, in relation to which Constitution is the people of California's action "unconstitutional"? Answer: the people of California's insistence that marriage is between one man and one woman runs against the Constitution imagined by the judge and supported by the Ruling Class. But that raises the most important questions: What obligation has anyone to obey that Constitution? Who ever agreed to it? No one even knows what it might say on any subject from one day to the next.

Are the words of the Constitution and laws to be understood according to the dictionary and grammar book? The 2010 confirmation hearing for Elena Kagan give us the Ruling Class' answer. On the second day of the hearing, Kagan engaged in what seemed like a scripted exchange with committee chairman Patrick Leahy (D-VT). Leahy said that some legal scholars believe that the Constitution is what the words in the document say, while others believe that those words' meaning must change with changing circumstances and needs, and thus that we have a "living Constitution." Kagan answered that she saw merit in both arguments, and that there are some cases in which the words mean what the dictionary says, and others in which it is necessary to find them compatible with what needs to be done, and that judges must decide on a case-by-case basis. This was supposed to show Kagan's moderation.

It takes but a little thought to realize that the power to decide when words mean what they say and when they do not is the power to do so whenever one wants, for whatever purpose. After all, the reason that

kings have traditionally opposed constitutions is that if a constitution has any meaning at all, it is some kind of restraint on government. But if government can decide that the constitution contains things that it does not, and allows things that it forbids, then adieu to the rule of law.

By 2010, some in the Ruling Class felt confident enough to dispense with the charade. Asked what in the Constitution allows Congress and the president to force every American to purchase health insurance, House Speaker Nancy Pelosi replied: "Are you kidding? Are you kidding?" It's no surprise, then, that lower court judges and bureaucrats take liberties with laws, regulations, and contracts. That's why legal words that say you are in the right avail you less in today's America than being on the right side of the persons who decide what they want those words to mean.

As the discretionary powers of officeholders and of their informal entourages have grown, the importance of policy and of law itself is declining, citizenship is becoming vestigial, and the American people are becoming ever more dependent—and, above all, more unequal.

Disaggregating and Dispiriting

The Ruling Class is keener to reform the American people's family and spiritual lives than their economic and civic ones. In no other areas is the Ruling Class' self-definition so definite, its contempt for opposition so patent, its *Kulturkampf* so open. It believes that the Christian family (and the Orthodox Jewish one, too) is rooted in and perpetuates the ignorance commonly called religion, divisive social prejudices, and repressive gender roles, that it is the greatest barrier to human progress because it looks to its very particular interest—often defined as mere coherence against outsiders who most often know better. Thus the family prevents its members from playing their proper roles in social reform. Worst of all, it reproduces itself.

Since marriage is the family's fertile seed, government at all levels, along with "mainstream" academics and media, have waged war on it. They legislate, regulate, and exhort in support not of "the family"— meaning married parents raising children—but rather of "families," meaning mostly households based on something other than marriage. The institution of no-fault divorce diminished the distinction between cohabitation and marriage, except that husbands are held financially responsible for the children they father, while out-of-wedlock fathers are not. The tax code penalizes marriage and forces those married couples who raise their own children to subsidize childcare for those who do not. Top Republicans and Democrats have also led society away from the very notion of marital fidelity by precept, as well as by parading their affairs. For example, in 1997, the Democratic administration's secretary of defense and the Republican Senate's majority leader (joined by the *New York Times* et al.) condemned the military's practice of punishing officers who had extramarital affairs. While the military had assumed that honoring marital vows is as fundamental to the integrity of its units as it is to that of society, consensus at the top declared that insistence on fidelity is "contrary to societal norms."

Not surprisingly, rates of marriage in America have decreased as out-of-wedlock births have increased. The biggest demographic consequence has been that about one in five of all households are women alone or with children, in which case they have about a four in ten chance of living in poverty. Since unmarried mothers often are or expect to be clients of government services, it is not surprising that they are among the Democratic Party's most faithful voters.

While our Ruling Class teaches that relationships

among men, women, and children are contingent, it also insists that the relationship between each of them and the state is fundamental. That is why people like Hillary Clinton have written law review articles and books advocating a direct relationship between the government and children, effectively abolishing the presumption of parental authority. Hence, whereas within living memory school nurses could not administer an aspirin to a child without the parents' consent, the people who run America's schools nowadays administer pregnancy tests and ship girls off to abortion clinics without the parents' knowledge. Parents are not allowed to object to what their children are taught. But the government may—and often does—object to how parents raise children. The Ruling Class' assumption is that what it mandates for children is correct ipso facto, while what parents do is potentially abusive. It only takes an anonymous accusation of abuse for parents to be taken away in handcuffs until they prove their innocence. Only sheer political weight (and in California, just barely) has preserved parents' right to home-school their children against the Ruling Class' desire to accomplish what Woodrow Wilson so yearned for: "to make young gentlemen as unlike their fathers as possible."

At stake are the most important questions: What is

the right way for human beings to live? By what standard is anything true or good? Who gets to decide
what? Implicit in Wilson's words and explicit in our
Ruling Class' actions is the dismissal of the answers
that most Americans would give to these questions.
The dismissal of the American people's intellectual,
spiritual, and moral substance is the very heart of
what our Ruling Class is about. Its principal article
of faith, its claim to the right to decide for others,
is precisely that it knows things scientifically, and
operates by standards beyond others' comprehension.
They claim moral authority as priests of what they
claim are ultimate truths.

While the unenlightened believe that man is created in the image and likeness of God, and that we are
subject to His and to His nature's laws, the enlightened *know* that we are products of evolution, driven
by chance, the environment, and the will to primacy.
While the unenlightened are stuck with the anti-
quated notion that ordinary human minds can reach
objective judgments about good and evil, better and
worse through reason, the enlightened *know* that all
such judgments are subjective, and that ordinary
people can no more be trusted with reason than they
can with guns. Because ordinary people will pervert
reason with ideology, religion, or interest, science is

"science" only in the "right" hands. Consensus among the right people is the only standard of truth. Facts and logic matter only insofar as proper authority acknowledges them.

That is why the Ruling Class is united and adamant about nothing so much as its right to pronounce definitive, "scientific" judgment on whatever it chooses. When the government declares, and its associated press echoes, that "scientists say" this or that, ordinary people—or, for that matter, scientists who *don't* say, or are not part of the Ruling Class—lose any right to see the information that went into what "scientists say." Thus, when Virginia's attorney general subpoenaed the data by which Professor Michael Mann had concluded, while paid by the state of Virginia, that the earth's temperatures are rising "like a hockey stick" from millennial stability—a conclusion on which billions of dollars worth of decisions were made—to investigate the possibility of fraud, the University of Virginia's faculty senate condemned any inquiry into "scientific endeavor that has satisfied peer review standards," claiming that demands for data "send a chilling message to scientists . . . and indeed scholars in any discipline." The *Washington Post* editorialized that the attorney general's demands for data amounted to "an assault on reason." A distinguished panel in Britain pronounced Mann and the others innocent, but the panel took no account of the accuracy of the disputed judgments, nor did it judge the data and reasoning that led to them. The fact that the "hockey stick" conclusion stands discredited and Mann and his associates are on record manipulating peer review, the fact that science-by-secret-data is an oxymoron, the very distinction between truth and error, all these matter far less to the Ruling Class than the distinction between themselves and those they rule.

By identifying science and reason with themselves, our rulers delegitimize opposition. Though they cannot prevent Americans from worshiping God, they can make it as socially disabling as smoking—to be done furtively and with a bad social conscience. Though they cannot make Americans wish they were Europeans, they continue to press upon this nation of refugees from the rest of the world the notion that Americans ought to live by "world standards." Each day, the Ruling Class produces new "studies" showing that one or another of Americans' habits is in need of reform, and that those Americans most resistant to reform are pitiably, perhaps criminally, wrong. Thus does it go about disaggregating and dispiriting the ruled.

CHAPTER 4

The Country Class

> *"Those that are good manners at the court are as*
> *ridiculous in the country as the behaviour of the*
> *country is most mockable at the court."*
>
> — WILLIAM SHAKESPEARE,
> *As You Like It*, (III.ii.45-8)

Describing America's Country Class is problematic because it is so heterogeneous. It has no privileged podiums, and it speaks with many voices, which are often inharmonious. It shares above all the desire to be rid of rulers it regards as inept and haughty. It defines itself practically in terms of reflexive reactions against the rulers' defining ideas and proclivities—e.g., ever-higher taxes and expanding government, subsidizing political favorites, social engineering, approval of abortion, etc. Many want to restore a way of life that has been largely superseded. The Country Class, like the Ruling Class, includes the professionally accomplished and the mediocre, the geniuses and the dolts. Demographically, the Country Class is the other side of the Ruling Class' coin: its most distinguishing characteristics are marriage, children, and religious practice. Politically, the Country Class may well be defined in terms of its lack of connection with government, and above all by attitudes opposite to those of the Ruling Class.

The Country Class is civil society, including both what Max Weber called *Gemeinschaft*, meaning the network of voluntary organizations that give communities their common element, and *Gesellschaft*, meaning commercial/professional relationships. But the Country Class is averse to having these relationships turned from their natural course by what Weber, had he thought of it, might have called *Machtschaft*, the tendency of rulers to undo voluntary organizations or to subordinate them to themselves, to channel civil society's economic activity to their own benefit, and to occupy the commanding heights of professional life. The Country Class is not anti-government, just nongovernmental. It views the way people live their lives as the result of countless private choices rather than as the consequence of someone else's master plan. It fears programs run by people whose titles sometimes includes the word "general," and who execute their program as if those in the way belonged to another nation.

Power Disconnect

Even as government officials or officers of major corporations whose decisions will have far-reaching effects, members of the Country Class do not think they have the right to do good in general by favoring one claimant over another. In their view, government owes equal treatment to its people, rather than action to correct what anyone perceives as imbalance or grievance. Hence, they tend to oppose special treatment, whether for corporations or for social categories. Rather than gaming government regulations, those in the Country Class try to stay as far from them as possible. Thus, the Supreme Court's 2005 decision in *Kelo v. City of New London*—which allows government to forcibly buy the private property of some and sell it to others who promise to produce more tax revenue, or whose purposes government deems worthier— reminded the Country Class that government is not the friend of the friendless. The Country Class knows that the government is there to serve the strong: the Ruling Class' members and supporters.

Negative orientation to privilege distinguishes the corporate officer who tries to keep his company from joining the Business Roundtable of large corporations who have close ties with government from the fellow in the next office. The former wants the company to grow by producing a better product at a lower cost. The latter wants it to grow by moving it as close to the feeding trough as possible. This sets apart the school-teacher who resents the union to which he is forced to belong for putting the union's interests above those of parents who want to choose their children's schools.

In general, the Country Class includes all those in stations high and low who are aghast at how relatively little honest work yields, by comparison with what just a little connection with the right bureaucracy can get you. It includes those who take the side of out-siders against insiders, of small institutions against large ones, of local government against those at the state or federal level. The Country Class is convinced that big business, big government, and big finance are linked as never before, and that ordinary people are more unequal than ever.

Members of the Country Class who want to rise in their professions through competence alone try at once to avoid the Ruling Class' rituals while guarding against infringing its prejudices. Averse to wheedling, they tend to think that exams should play a major role in getting or advancing in jobs, that records of performance—including academic ones—should be matters of public record, and that professional disputes should be settled by open argument. For such people, the Supreme Court's 2009 decision in *Ricci v. DeStefano*, upholding the right of firefighters to be promoted according to the results of a professional exam, revived the hope that competence may sometimes still trump political connections. But that hope becomes slimmer as government becomes fatter.

The Country Class thinks that individuals, and in special circumstances local elected officials—not Federal or state bureaucrats—have the right to decide what kind of light bulbs a home should have, how much water should flow from a shower nozzle, what kind of toilet you should install. Country Class people are not happy with automobiles designed to meet ever more regulations, which have made these vehicles virtually impossible to fix without specialized equipment run by technicians. Losing the capacity to get your own car going means losing some more autonomy, becoming further subjected to the workings of a "system" that seems to produce mainly less freedom and more dependency on people less and less like yourself.

Equality and Standards

Whereas rejection of human equality is the Ruling Class' defining feature, most of the Country Class believes that all men are created equal. While some believe in human equality and abhor privilege for religious or ideological reasons, many more do so, as it were, out of Newton's First Law of Motion: "bodies in motion tend to remain in motion." Equality is so fundamental to everything American, so ingrained in how we regard and deal with one another, and the notion that America is classless is so fundamental to our self-conception, that unless someone is taught, very carefully taught, that he is superior or inferior to others, he is likely to agree, without much thought, that the Declaration of Independence is right: "all men *are created equal*." Presuming equality made it difficult for the Country Class to notice that a class of people was being carefully taught the contrary.

Nothing has set the Country Class apart, defined it, made it conscious of itself, and given it whatever coherence it has, so much as the Ruling Class' insistence that people other than themselves are intellectually—and hence otherwise humanly—inferior. Persons who were brought up to believe themselves as worthy as anyone, who manage their own lives to their own satisfaction, naturally resent politicians of both parties who say that the issues of modern life are too complex for anyone but themselves. Most are insulted by the Ruling Class' dismissal of opposition as mere "anger and frustration"—an imputation of stupidity—while others just scoff at the claim that the Ruling Class' bureaucratic language demonstrates superior intelligence. A few ask: Since when and by what right does intelligence trump human equality? Moreover, if the politicians are so smart, why have they made life worse? But the fundamental, enduring question is: what are the proper standards of right and wrong, better and worse? The Country Class is convinced that our rulers are wrongly oriented.

While the Ruling Class prods Americans to become more like Europeans, and talks as if America should move *up* to "world standards," the Country Class believes that America's ways are superior to the rest of the world's, and regards most of mankind as less free, less prosperous, and less virtuous than Americans. Thus, while the Country Class delights in croissants and thinks Toyota's factory methods are worth imitating, it dislikes the idea of adhering to "world standards."

This class also takes part in the U.S. armed forces, body and soul: nearly all the enlisted, non-commissioned officers and officers under flag rank belong to this class in every measurable way. Few vote for the Democratic Party. You do not doubt that you are amid the Country Class rather than the Ruling Class when the American flag passes by or "God Bless America" is sung after seven innings of baseball, and most people show reverence. The same people wince at the National Football League's plaintive renditions of "The Star-Spangled Banner."

Unlike the Ruling Class, the Country Class does not share a single intellectual orthodoxy, set of tastes, or ideal lifestyle. Some parts of the Country Class now follow the stars and the music out of Nashville, Tennessee and Branson, Missouri—entertainment complexes larger than Hollywood's—because since the 1970s most of Hollywood's products have appealed more to the tastes of the Ruling Class and its underclass clients than to those of large percentages of Americans. The same goes for "popular" music and television. For some in the Country Class, Christian radio and TV are the lodestone of sociopolitical taste, while the very secular Fox News serves the same purpose for others. While symphonies and opera houses around the country, as well as the television and radio stations that broadcast them, are firmly in the Ruling Class' hands, a considerable part of the Country Class appreciates these things for their own sake.

Standards and Separation

The home-school movement—the Country Class' signature cultural venture—shows the reasons why diversely motivated components thereof want to reclaim responsibility for an essential part of human life that was unnaturally taken from them, how they are going about it, and how that is making the Country Class more conscious of itself.

The Census Bureau reports that by 1999, 1.7 percent of American children were schooled at home, and that by 2007 the proportion had reached 2.9 percent. By 2010 it was well over 3 percent, and growing ever faster. Parents choose home-schooling for reasons that differ little from those that led another 4 percent of Americans to pay for private schooling, and 7 percent to pay for religious (mostly Catholic) schooling. These are the same reasons why parents of public-school children clamor for charter schools. In short, one out of seven sets of parents has already abandoned the public schools, and many more wish they could. According to a 2007 U.S. Department of Education survey, 68 percent of parents who chose home-schooling "were dissatisfied with academic instruction" in the public schools; 85 percent objected to the public schools' "social environments" (the dominant culture); and 72 percent wanted to be in charge of "religious and moral instruction." So, by taking children out of public schools, or wishing to do it, millions of parents recognize that the Ruling Class' idea of education is different from theirs. That is why they try to take back responsibility for education (home schools take back all; charters schools just a little).

Small, rural public schools are a special case because parents can influence the content and standards of education. They typically have the lowest per-pupil expenditures (Utah spends only $5,257 per pupil) and produce America's highest SAT scores, while the states that spend the most produce the lowest. If one divides the number of per capita dollars spent by any jurisdiction by the total SAT points scored by students in those jurisdictions, Utah gets 2.1 SAT points per dollar, while the District of Columbia, which spends three times as much as Utah, gets only .07. The Country Class has learned through bitter experience, and is ever less shy about the fact that parents have proven to be better guides to educating the next generation than have highly credentialed and paid experts wielding government power.

The content of home-school curricula, though very diverse in detail, stresses first the basics of language and math, and then the classics in science, literature, music, or history, even as the Ruling Class abandons them. Home-schoolers beyond the earliest grades seldom have textbooks. This alone saves them from growing up on a diet of simple sentences, cartoon characters, and straw-man arguments, never mind from having the latest education fads pushed upon them. Rather, they cut their intellectual teeth on original texts filled with complex syntax and arguments. In science and math, having to solve the problem is their responsibility alone, not "the team's," as in public school. And while credentialed educators assign books such as *I, Rigoberta Menchú*, a pseudo-biography of a pseudo-revolutionary, home-school moms don't know any better than to read Shakespeare with the kids. The result is that SAT scores for home-schoolers hover around the eightieth percentile. How did those dumb, violent racists achieve results like that?

Before the internet, home-school families struggled to get good materials. There was a run on the

McGuffey reader series. But the internet has enabled physically separated people to draw from publishing houses around the country, and has put these in contact with a growing market. Old books are being reprinted and good new ones written. Just as important, home-school parents routinely learn from others' experiences and pool resources to teach subjects that some parents know and others don't. They also organize sports and social events. An organic network has grown, a flourishing one at that, which, dispensing with Max Weber, we recognize simply as civil society.

Few in this part of the Country Class have any illusion that retreating into private associations will long save their families from societal influences made to order to discredit their ways. Day after day, the Ruling Class' imputations—racist, stupid, prone to violence, incapable of running things—but like artillery cover for the advance of legislation and regulation to restrict and delegitimize. There is no escape from the conflict between the classes.

CHAPTER 5

Agendas Revolutionary?

"Corcyra gave the first . . . of the reprisals exacted by the governed, who had never experienced equitable treatment or indeed aught but insolence from their rulers . . . of the savage and pitiless excesses into which men who had begun the struggle, not in a class but in a party spirit, were hurried by their ungovernable passions. In the confusion into which life was now thrown . . . human nature . . . gladly showed itself ungoverned in passion, above respect for justice, and the enemy of all superiority. Indeed, men too often take upon themselves in the prosecution of their revenge to set the example of doing away with those general laws to which all alike can look for salvation in adversity, instead of allowing them to subsist against the day of danger when their aid may be required."

— THUCYDIDES

Our rulers believe it is right for the ruled to shut up and obey, or at most cut little deals for themselves. The ruled believe they have a God-given right to self-governance. The Ruling Class has been revolutionizing America, to the Country Class' distaste. Though the Country Class had long argued against revolutionary changes, it now faces the uncomfortable question common to all who have had revolutionary changes imposed on them: are we now to accept what was done to us just because it was done? Because each side embodies itself in the issues, concessions by one side to another on any issue tend to discredit that side's view of itself. Once such states of tensions are reached, any ordinary controversy can spiral into ever more destructive revolutionary acts. What Thucydides showed two and a half millennia ago, what mankind has learned bitterly countless times since, most recently in France and Russia, is that revolutions loose passions and generate the power to slake them. In the American Revolution, only extraordinary statesmanship kept party spirit from spiraling as it did elsewhere.

Revolutions are deadly. And yet America is not in a position to avoid at least a period of strife over essential things. Americans beset by noxious rulers long ago lost the option available to Roger Williams, who took his non-conformists out of Massachusetts to found Rhode Island, or to Brigham Young, who took his Mormons from oppression in New York to freedom in Utah. The rulers of the day let them go. Today's Ruling Class knows no reason why it should limit its intrusions into the Country Class' life. Anyone intent on stopping any given intrusion soon finds himself confronted by its entire power—agencies armed with powers backed by studies and megaphoned by the media. Whoever would not submit is forced to confront the premises of the Ruling Class, its pretense to power—to challenge its entire conception of man, of right and wrong, its very legitimacy. Merely thinking that way is revolutionary—never mind acting on that basis.

Because of its diverse nature, the Country Class has no agenda such as the Ruling Class has. But every Country Class sector that pushes back against the Ruling Class' pressures has been forced into a similar line of reasoning, from which arise the stark alternatives of submission or of a principled effort against the Ruling Class as a whole. Business groups of all kinds hire lobbyists to lessen the impact of regulation and taxes. Anti-tax groups agitate. Private groups fight abortion at every level.

Pro-family groups have been successful in passing state constitutional amendments stating what no one would have disputed—that marriage means joining one man and one woman. Religious groups have tried, with much less success, to limit the U.S. government's denigration of Christianity and Orthodox Judaism. The Federalist Society has done exemplary work to reintroduce into our legal profession the concept that words have meaning. But if we call such defensive efforts "agendas," then what do we call the Ruling Class' objectives and activities in each of these fields? The Ruling Class' proximate objectives—allowing only such economic activities as are part of its plans, finishing the transformation of America into an administrative state, reducing American families to Swedish levels of intellectual and moral subordination to government "science" of all sources of reason or authority—are based on its claim of superiority and its denigration of lower beings, which it shouts from the housetops. Having noticed this, more and more Country Class activists realize that they must accompany concrete proposals with principled refusal of the Ruling Class' claim to authority. "Who the hell do they think they are?" is full of revolutionary implications.

The Country Class' agenda arises from this question:

what will it actually take, what is to be done, to reclaim the Country Class way of American life?

Here a brief but essential digression. "What is to be done?" is the title of Lenin's most important paper—the blueprint not just for the Communist Party that bloodily ruined Russia, but also for much of modern government. Lenin turned his back on the people because Lenin's Bolshevik faction had become frustrated by the Russian people's coolness to its plans, and began crafting the Communist Party into an organization of *professionals*. Note well that political activities by citizens on one hand, and on the other by professionals of power, are as different as night and day. Understanding the clash between America's Ruling Class and Country Class requires starting from the fact that our Ruling Class is largely professional—in the sense that ruling is itself its business (the Stanford undergraduate who complained to the *Daily* had no doubt of that)—while the Country Class is largely not. But fully understanding the clash means knowing that the Country Class cannot prevail by forming an alternative Ruling Class. Much of the world is saddled with many ruling classes that alternate on the people's backs.

Transcending intellectually the mild defensive measures that each of the Country Class' sectors have taken heretofore is itself revolutionary. Making technocratic arguments against redistributive economics, against paying for things no one would buy, for feeding political favorites, for unpayable deficits, is easy—too easy, because the targets are so obvious: the upper tiers of the U.S. economy are now nothing but networks of special deals with one part of government or another. But what would it take to undo this interpenetration of government and business, this network of subsidies, preferences, and regulations so thick and deep? The people "at the table" receive and recycle into politics so much money that independent businesspeople cannot hope to undo any given regulation or grant of privilege. All of us are beneficiaries, in some way. How to untangle such a corrupt knot? Just as no manufacturer can hope to reduce the subsidies that raise his fuel costs, no set of doctors can shield themselves from the increased costs and bureaucracy resulting from government mandates.

The Country Class can hope to cut that knot only by mobilizing itself against it on a principled, moral basis—understanding that the system of privileges is dishonest, and being willing to dispense with whatever threads of it they hold. "The sum of good government," said Thomas Jefferson, is not taking "from the mouth of labor the bread it has earned." For government to advantage some at others' expense, said he, "is to violate arbitrarily the first principle of association." Is that true or false? If the Country Class concludes that is false or passé, it will bow heads further, and pull the yoke. If it is true, then it can slough off a whole lot of economic dross at once. How one might do this is another matter. But the revolutionary choice for the Country Class has to be: are you willing to upset the apple cart from which you get your ration of apples?

Any member of the Country Class who thinks about it knows that bureaucrats who disempowered neighborhood school boards, while turning the governments of towns, counties, and states into conduits for federal mandates, are public employees, whom he pays, and who are supposed to serve him. Following orders and paid from above, these public employees draft the millions of pages of new regulations that issue from government and which (especially the paperwork provisions) make criminals of us all. The fact that public employees are almost always paid more and have more generous benefits than the private sector people whose taxes support them only sharpens the sense among many in the Country Class that they now work for public employees rather than the other way around. This is what happens in many European countries, and has happened in the state of California.

But how to reverse the roles? How can voters regain control of government?

The bureaucrats' powers to tell us what kinds of light bulbs or cars we can use, or how many hoops we must jump through before doing any number of things, derive from laws, each of which is based on the same premise: ordinary people, as consumers, landowners, or citizens, are incompetent to make such decisions. The Country Class has figured out that it makes far more sense to attack the premise of the laws than the bureaucracy. This logical conclusion, though revolutionary, is easy. Doing something about it, however, is fraught with difficulties.

Restoring localities' traditional powers over schools, including standards, curriculum, and prayer, would take repudiating two generations of Supreme Court rulings. So would the restoration of traditional police powers over behavior in public places. Bringing public employee unions to heel is only incidentally a matter of cutting pay and benefits. As self-governance is crimped primarily by the powers of government personified in its employees, restoring it involves primarily deciding that any number of functions now performed, and the professional specialists who perform them (e.g., social workers), are superfluous or worse. Explaining to oneself and one's neighbors why such functions and personnel do more harm than good, while the Ruling Class brings its powers to bear to discredit you, is a very revolutionary thing to do.

America's pro-family movement is a reaction to the Ruling Class' challenges: emptying marriage of legal sanction, promoting abortion, and progressively excluding parents from their children's education. Americans reacted to these challenges primarily by sorting themselves out. Close friendships, and above all, marriages, became rarer between persons who think well of divorce, abortion, and government authority over children and those who do not. The home-school movement, for which the internet became the great facilitator, involves not only each family educating its own children, but also extensive and growing social, intellectual, and spiritual contact among like-minded persons. In short, the part of the Country Class that is most concerned with family matters has taken on something of a biological identity. But to defend it is to attack its attackers.

The Ruling Class' manifold efforts to discredit and drive worship of God out of public life—not even in the Soviet Union were students arrested for wearing crosses or praying, or reading the Bible on school property, as some U.S. localities have done in response to Supreme Court rulings—convinced many among the vast majority of Americans who believe and pray that today's regime is hostile to the most important things of all. Every December, they are reminded that the Ruling Class deems the very word "Christmas" to be offensive. Every time they try to manifest their religious identity in public affairs, they are deluged by accusations of being "American Taliban" trying to set up a "theocracy." Let members of the Country Class object to anything the Ruling Class says or does, and likely as not their objection will be characterized as "religious"—that is to say, irrational, not to be considered on a par with the "science" of which the Ruling Class is the sole legitimate interpreter. Because aggressive, intolerant secularism is the moral and intellectual basis of the Ruling Class' claim to rule, resistance to that rule, whether to the immorality of economic subsidies and privileges, or to the violation of the principle of equal treatment under equal law, or to its seizure of children's education, must deal with secularism's intellectual and moral core. This lies beyond the boundaries of politics, as the term is commonly understood.

CHAPTER 6

How?

"Republican candidates should happily accept {the Tea Party's} support while sticking to their own views and stands, whatever they are."

— PEGGY NOONAN,
The Wall Street Journal, July 30, 2010

"As soon as they get here, we need to co-opt them."

— TRENT LOTT,
Republican Majority Leader-turned lobbyist

arly-twenty-first-century American political struggles transcend the Democratic—but mostly the Republican—Party. As we have noted, only a fourth of those who vote Republican are happy about it. Few who will vote Republican in 2010 and 2012 will do so for the sake of Republican "views and stands, whatever they are." In short, the Republican Party lives by default, because, in the short term, the Country Class has no alternative but to channel its political efforts through Republicans. But generic Republican "views and stands" and candidates have been losers. As it was before, and has been after Ronald Reagan, the Republican Party has zero claim to the Country Class' trust because it does not live to represent the Country Class. Rather, those who have dominated the Party have served themselves and co-opted into the Ruling Class persons whom the electorate elected to oppose that class. The few who tried to make the Republican Party the representative of Republican voters, the party treated as rebels. The party helped defeat Barry Goldwater. When it failed to stop Ronald Reagan, it saddled his and subsequent Republican administrations with establishmentarians who, under the Bush family, repudiated Reagan's principles as much as they could. Barack Obama exaggerated in charging that Republicans had driven the country "into the ditch" all alone. But they had a big, unforgettable hand in it. Republican voters, never mind the larger Country Class, have little reason to believe that the party is on their side. Republicans who imagine that the Country Class votes they will receive in 2010 and perhaps 2012 are for them, rather than against the Ruling Class, will have rude awakenings.

Because, in the long run, the Country Class will not support a party that intends to co-opt the people's elected representatives into the Ruling Class, those Republican politicians who really want to represent it will either reform the party in an unmistakable manner or start a new one, as Whigs like Abraham Lincoln started the Republican Party in the 1850s.

But the name of the party that will represent America's Country Class is far less important than what, precisely, it will represent, and how it will go about representing it. That is because, although the Country Class lacks its own political vehicle—and perhaps the coherence to establish one—it does not take much to realize that the massive Country Class well-nigh demands to be represented by the opposite of those who have ruled America for the past generation, that that demand will call forth supply under whatever name, and that, sooner rather than later, America's two-party system, responding to the American people's indigestion of what the Ruling Class has forced upon it, will produce Congresses and Presidents pledged *somehow* against it.

Partisan Politics

De facto, this would mean that another party would be in the position to rule more or less at will. But partisan logic leads to such majorities and Presidents becoming the mirror image of U.S. Democrats, or of even more unsavory foreign parties. Yet with the Democratic Party having transformed itself into a unit with near-European discipline, what other antidote is there to government by one party but government by a rival party at least as disciplined? But this logic, though all too familiar to most of the world, has always been foreign to America, and naturally leads further in the direction toward which the Ruling Class has led. Any victorious Country Party would have to be wise and skillful indeed to avoid that.

That is because, to defend the Country Class, to break down the Ruling Class' presumptions, any serious political force has no choice but to imitate the Democrats, at least in some ways and for a while. Consider: the Ruling Class denies its opponents' legitimacy. Seldom does a Democratic official or member of the Ruling Class speak on public affairs without reiterating the litany of his class' claim to authority, contrasting it with opponents who are either uninformed, stupid, racist, shills for business, violent, fundamentalist, or all of the above. They do this in the hope that opponents, hearing no other characterizations of themselves and no authoritative voice discrediting the Ruling Class, will be dispirited. For the Country Class to seriously contend for self-governance, the political party that represents it will have to do more than discredit such patent frauds as ethanol mandates, the pretense that taxes can control "climate change," and the outrage of banning God from public life. The tame truism that there are extremists on all sides becomes effectively an apology for whatever sins the rulers impute to the people.

More importantly, such a serious party would have to attack the Ruling Class' fundamental claims to its superior intellect and morality in ways that dispirit the target and hearten one's own. The Democrats having set the rules of modern politics; opponents who want electoral success are obliged to follow them to some extent.

Moreover, any victorious Country Party must somehow stop the Ruling Class' growing habit of prosecuting prominent political opponents—a habit most ruinous to any body politic. Prosecutions of aides to Presidents and Vice Presidents that ruin their personal lives for serving their policies in lieu of proper

motions of impeachment of the principles is the sort
of stuff that naturally invites retaliation. Thucydides'
account of Corcyra's self-destruction begins precisely
with the escalation of this sort of tit for tat. Cycles of
vengeance spiral in only one direction. And yet, were
a victorious Country Party so magnanimous as to
simply ignore the persons and processes by which the
Ruling Class has criminalized political differences,
it would grant them an easement. Criminalizing the
criminalization of politics is akin to the wonder performed by Aeschylus' *Eumenides*, which turned revenge
into law—high statesmanship.

Just as difficult and just as un-amenable to mere
self-restraint would be the task of re-training rulers
grown accustomed to treating their own desires as
law, and henceforth to respect law's limits. Suppose
that the Country Party were to capture Congress, the
Presidency, and most statehouses. What then would
it do? Especially if its majority were slim, it would be
tempted to follow the Democrats' plan of 2009–10,
namely to write its wish list of reforms into law,
regardless of the Constitution, and enact them by partisan majorities supported by interest groups that gain
from them, while continuing to vilify the other side.
Whatever effect this might have, it surely would not
be to make America safe for self-governance, because

by carrying out its own "revolution from above" to reverse the Ruling Class' previous "revolution from above," it would have made that ruinous practice standard in America. Moreover, a revolution designed at party headquarters would be antithetical to the Country Class' diversity, as well as to the American founders' legacy.

But how could the Country Party, without being lawless, make the Ruling Class feel that failing to take seriously the Constitution and the laws has hard consequences for them? How, for example, to remind America of, and to drive home to the Ruling Class, Lincoln's lesson that trifling with the Constitution for the most heartfelt of motives destroys its protections for all?

What if a Country Class majority in both houses of Congress were to co-sponsor a "Bill of Attainder to deprive Nancy Pelosi, Barack Obama, and other persons of liberty and property without further process of law for having violated the following ex-post-facto law . . ." and larded this constitutional monstrosity with an Article III Section 2 exemption from federal court review? When the affected members of the Ruling Class asked where Congress gets the authority to pass a bill every word of which is contrary to the Constitution, they would be confronted, publicly, with House Speaker Nancy Pelosi's answer to a question on

Congress' constitutional authority to mandate individuals to purchase certain kinds of insurance: "Are you kidding? Are you kidding?" The point having been made, the Country Party could dispense with passage, and lead public discussions around the country on why even the noblest purposes cannot be allowed to trump the Constitution.

Cutting

What might a prudent Country Party do to achieve the Country Class' inherently revolutionary objectives in a manner consistent with the Constitution and with its own peaceful diversity? Though legislation, some of the draconian kind, would be the indispensable tool for cutting away the parasitic growths on America's body politic, most would serve to remove obstacles to civil society, to instruct, to reintroduce into American life ways and habits that had been cast aside. Yet any and all legislation is easier than getting people to take up the responsibilities of citizens, fathers, and entrepreneurs.

Reducing the taxes that most Americans resent requires eliminating the network of subsidies to millions of other Americans that these taxes finance, and eliminating the jobs of government employees who administer them. Eliminating that network is practical, if at all, if done simultaneously, both because subsidies are morally wrong and economically counterproductive, and because the country cannot afford the practice in general. The electorate is likely to cut off millions of government clients, high and low, only if its choice is between no economic privilege for anyone, and ratifying government's role as the arbiter of all our fortunes. The same goes for government grants to and contracts with so-called nonprofit institutions or non-governmental organizations. The case against all arrangements by which the government favors some groups of citizens is easier to make than that against any such arrangement.

Cutting the size of government is as essential to the body politic's health as a weight-reduction program is to restoring any human body that excess has caused to degrade into obesity. Just as someone who is serious about his health asks, "Do I need cupcakes at all? Didn't I get along even better before I made them part of my life?," proof of the Country Class' seriousness is whether it asks, "Do we really need the National Endowments for the Arts and Humanities? Didn't we get along perfectly well before we had the Corporation for Public Broadcasting? Do we really want

Social Security to provide a living for drug addicts and alcoholics? If America was better educated before we established a Department of Education than it has been since, why do we continue to have such a department?" Reducing agencies' budgets is unserious. If a job should be done and the agency is doing it, why cut? But if it is not, why not abolish?

Rehab

Yet shedding fat is the easy part. Restoring atrophied muscles is harder. Re-enabling the body to do elementary tasks takes yet more concentration. Does the Country Class really want to govern itself, or is it just whining for milder taskmasters? How ready, willing, and able is the Country Class to do more than vote every couple of years for people about whom it does not know and on issues it does not care to understand? Above all, how many in the Country Class are ready, willing, and able to run local affairs? Just as in all cases of rehab, everything depends on how much the patient puts into his well-being.

If self-governance means anything, it means that those who exercise government power must depend on elections. The shorter the electoral leash, the likelier an official is to have his chain yanked by voters, and the more truly republican the government is. Yet to subject the modern administrative state's agencies to electoral control would require ordinary citizens to take an interest in any number of technical matters. Law can require environmental regulators or insurance commissioners, or judges or auditors to be elected. But only citizens' discernment and vigilance could make these officials good. Only citizens' understanding of and commitment to law can possibly reverse the patent disregard for the Constitution and statutes that has permeated American life.

But if self-governance means anything, it means, as Aristotle wrote so long ago, "ruling and being ruled in turn." This is obviously the antithesis of the modern notion that government—transformative government, at that—is the business of professionals. Lenin's commitment to professional government grew while he was exiled in Switzerland, where, at the time, all matters of any importance were decided by popular referendum, where officials were ordinary citizens and ordinary citizens were officials. Switzerland has not changed much. A century ago there was another country where, though referenda were not much used, officials were citizens and citizens officials—the United States of America. But here, much has changed. The grandparents of today's Americans (132 million in 1940) had opportunities to serve on 117,000 school boards. To exercise responsibilities comparable to their grandparents', today's 310 million Americans would have to radically decentralize the mere 15,000 districts into which public school children are now concentrated. A century ago, Americans also governed themselves by taking responsibility for basic services such as water, sanitation, and electricity. Local ordinances set different tones of life.

Were the legal and institutional barriers to doing so removed, would today's Country Class be willing to shoulder the responsibilities that their grandparents bore as proud badges of American citizenship? Would some in the Country Class take the (considerable) pains to explain why credentialed experts in any number of fields either should be dismissed because they do not know better, or if they do, should be retained as advisers to elected officials? Would enough members of the Country Class pay enough attention? This would involve a level of political articulation of the body politic far beyond voting in elections every two years.

The Odds

In this clash, the Ruling Class holds most of the cards: it holds strong defensive positions and is well represented by the Democratic Party. Because it has established itself as the fount of authority, its primacy is based on habits of deference. Breaking them, establishing other founts of authority and other ways of doing things, would involve far more than electoral politics—of which the Country Class has not yet shown the capacity. Its greatest difficulty—aside from being outnumbered two to one—will be to argue, against the grain of reality, that the revolution it continues to press upon America is sustainable. Its management of more and more things has left fewer and fewer people happy. It may win some elections by arguing that its opponents are stupid, etc. Thus it may hold on to power for a while. But America's majority long since withdrew its confidence from a class that has earned, and has no way of shedding, the image of pretentious, incompetent losers.

For the Country Class, winning elections will be the easy part. Avoiding bitter partisan government on the one hand, and co-option into the Ruling Class on the other, will be harder. Harder yet will be sweeping away a half century's accretions of bad habits. Taking care to preserve the good among them is hard enough; establishing, even reestablishing, a set of better institutions and habits is much harder. The Country Class' greatest difficulty will be to enable a revolution to take place without imposing it. America has been imposed on enough.

THE DECLARATION OF INDEPENDENCE

IN CONGRESS, JULY 4, 1776

*The unanimous Declaration of the thirteen
united States of America*

When in the Course of human events it becomes necessary for one people to dissolve the political bands
which have connected them with another and to
assume among the powers of the earth, the separate
and equal station to which the Laws of Nature and
of Nature's God entitle them, a decent respect to the
opinions of mankind requires that they should declare
the causes which impel them to the separation.

We hold these truths to be self-evident, that all men
are created equal, that they are endowed by their Cre-
ator with certain unalienable Rights, that among these
are Life, Liberty and the pursuit of Happiness. That to
secure these rights, Governments are instituted among
Men, deriving their just powers from the consent of

the governed. That whenever any Form of Government becomes destructive of these ends, it is the Right of the People to alter or to abolish it, and to institute new Government, laying its foundation on such principles and organizing its powers in such form, as to them shall seem most likely to effect their Safety and Happiness. Prudence, indeed, will dictate that Governments long established should not be changed for light and transient causes; and accordingly all experience hath shewn that mankind are more disposed to suffer, while evils are sufferable, than to right themselves by abolishing the forms to which they are accustomed. But when a long train of abuses and usurpations, pursuing invariably the same Object evinces a design to reduce them under absolute Despotism, it is their right, it is their duty, to throw off such Government, and to provide new Guards for their future security. Such has been the patient sufferance of these Colonies; and such is now the necessity which constrains them to alter their former Systems of Government. The history of the present King of Great Britain is a history of repeated injuries and usurpations, all having in direct object the establishment of an absolute Tyranny over these States. To prove this, let Facts be submitted to a candid world.

He has refused his Assent to Laws, the most wholesome and necessary for the public good.

He has forbidden his Governors to pass Laws of immediate and pressing importance, unless suspended in their operation till his Assent should be obtained; and when so suspended, he has utterly neglected to attend to them.

He has refused to pass other Laws for the accommodation of large districts of people, unless those people would relinquish the right of Representation in the Legislature, a right inestimable to them and formidable to tyrants only.

He has called together legislative bodies at places unusual, uncomfortable, and distant from the depository of their Public Records, for the sole purpose of fatiguing them into compliance with his measures.

He has dissolved Representative Houses repeatedly, for opposing with manly firmness his invasions on the rights of the people.

He has refused for a long time, after such dissolutions, to cause others to be elected, whereby the Legislative Powers, incapable of Annihilation, have returned to the People at large for their exercise; the State remaining in the meantime exposed to all the dangers of invasion from without, and convulsions within.

He has endeavoured to prevent the population of these States; for that purpose obstructing the Laws for Naturalization of Foreigners; refusing to pass others to encourage their migrations hither, and raising the conditions of new Appropriations of Lands.

He has obstructed the Administration of Justice by refusing his Assent to Laws for establishing Judiciary Powers.

He has made Judges dependent on his Will alone for the tenure of their offices, and the amount and payment of their salaries.

He has erected a multitude of New Offices, and sent hither swarms of Officers to harass our people and eat out their substance.

He has kept among us, in times of peace, Standing Armies without the Consent of our legislatures.

He has affected to render the Military independent of and superior to the Civil Power.

He has combined with others to subject us to a jurisdiction foreign to our constitution, and unacknowledged by our laws; giving his Assent to their Acts of pretended Legislation.

For quartering large bodies of armed troops among us.

For protecting them, by a mock Trial, from punishment for any Murders which they should commit on the Inhabitants of these States.

For cutting off our Trade with all parts of the world.

For imposing Taxes on us without our Consent.

For depriving us, in many cases, of the benefit of Trial by Jury.

For transporting us beyond Seas to be tried for pretended offences.

For abolishing the free System of English Laws in a neighbouring Province, establishing therein an Arbitrary government, and enlarging its Boundaries so as to render it at once an example and fit instrument for introducing the same absolute rule into these Colonies.

For taking away our Charters, abolishing our most valuable Laws and altering fundamentally the Forms of our Governments.

For suspending our own Legislatures, and declaring themselves invested with power to legislate for us in all cases whatsoever.

He has abdicated Government here, by declaring us out of his Protection and waging War against us.

He has plundered our seas, ravaged our coasts, burnt our towns, and destroyed the lives of our people.

He is at this time transporting large Armies of foreign Mercenaries to compleat the works of death, desolation, and tyranny, already begun with circumstances of Cruelty & Perfidy scarcely paralleled in the most barbarous ages, and totally unworthy of the

Head of a civilized nation.

He has constrained our fellow Citizens taken Captive on the high Seas to bear Arms against their Country, to become the executioners of their friends and Brethren, or to fall themselves by their Hands.

He has excited domestic insurrections amongst us, and has endeavoured to bring on the inhabitants of our frontiers, the merciless Indian Savages whose known rule of warfare, is an undistinguished destruction of all ages, sexes and conditions.

In every stage of these Oppressions We have Petitioned for Redress in the most humble terms: Our repeated Petitions have been answered only by repeated injury. A Prince, whose character is thus marked by every act which may define a Tyrant, is unfit to be the ruler of a free people.

Nor have We been wanting in attentions to our British brethren. We have warned them from time to time of attempts by their legislature to extend an unwarrantable jurisdiction over us. We have reminded them of the circumstances of our emigration and settlement here. We have appealed to their native justice and magnanimity, and we have conjured them by the ties of our common kindred to disavow these usurpations, which would inevitably interrupt our connections and correspondence. They too have been deaf to the voice of justice and of consanguinity. We must, therefore, acquiesce in the necessity, which denounces our Separation, and hold them, as we hold the rest of mankind, Enemies in War, in Peace Friends.

We, therefore, the Representatives of the united States of America, in General Congress, Assembled, appealing to the Supreme Judge of the world for the rectitude of our intentions, do, in the Name, and by Authority of the good People of these Colonies, solemnly publish and declare, that these united Colonies are, and of Right ought to be, Free and Independent States, that they are Absolved from all Allegiance to the British Crown, and that all political connection between them and the State of Great Britain, is and ought to be totally dissolved; and that as Free and Independent States, they have full Power to levy War, conclude Peace, contract Alliances, establish Commerce, and to do all other Acts and Things which Independent States may of right do. And for the support of this Declaration, with a firm reliance on the protection of Divine Providence, we mutually pledge to each other our Lives, our Fortunes, and our sacred Honor.

John Hancock

NEW HAMPSHIRE:
Josiah Bartlett, William Whipple, Matthew Thornton

MASSACHUSETTS:
John Hancock, Samuel Adams, John Adams, Robert Treat Paine, Elbridge Gerry

RHODE ISLAND:
Stephen Hopkins, William Ellery

CONNECTICUT:
Roger Sherman, Samuel Huntington, William Williams, Oliver Wolcott

NEW YORK:
William Floyd, Philip Livingston, Francis Lewis, Lewis Morris

NEW JERSEY:
Richard Stockton, John Witherspoon, Francis Hopkinson, John Hart, Abraham Clark

PENNSYLVANIA:
Robert Morris, Benjamin Rush, Benjamin Franklin, John Morton, George Clymer, James Smith, George Taylor, James Wilson, George Ross

DELAWARE:
Caesar Rodney, George Read, Thomas McKean

MARYLAND:
Samuel Chase, William Paca, Thomas Stone, Charles Carroll of Carrollton

VIRGINIA:
George Wythe, Richard Henry Lee, Thomas Jefferson, Benjamin Harrison, Thomas Nelson, Jr., Francis Lightfoot Lee, Carter Braxton

NORTH CAROLINA:
William Hooper, Joseph Hewes, John Penn

SOUTH CAROLINA:
Edward Rutledge, Thomas Heyward, Jr., Thomas Lynch, Jr., Arthur Middleton

GEORGIA:
Button Gwinnett, Lyman Hall, George Walton

THE CONSTITUTION

We the People of the United States, in Order to form a more perfect Union, establish Justice, insure domestic Tranquility, provide for the common defence, promote the general Welfare, and secure the Blessings of Liberty to ourselves and our Posterity, do ordain and establish this Constitution for the United States of America.

ARTICLE 1.

- SECTION 1

All legislative Powers herein granted shall be vested in a Congress of the United States, which shall consist of a Senate and House of Representatives.

- SECTION 2

The House of Representatives shall be composed of Members chosen every second Year by the People of the several States, and the Electors in each State shall have the Qualifications requisite for Electors of the most numerous Branch of the State Legislature.

No Person shall be a Representative who shall not have attained to the Age of twenty-five Years, and been seven Years a Citizen of the United States, and who shall not, when elected, be an Inhabitant of that State in which he shall be chosen.

Representatives and direct Taxes shall be apportioned among the several States which may be included within this Union, according to their respective Numbers, which shall be determined by adding to the whole Number of free Persons, including those bound to Service for a Term of Years, and excluding Indians not taxed, three-fifths of all other Persons.

The actual Enumeration shall be made within three Years after the first Meeting of the Congress of the United States, and within every subsequent Term of ten Years, in such Manner as they shall by Law direct. The Number of Representatives shall not exceed one for every thirty Thousand, but each State shall have at Least one Representative; and until such enumeration shall be made, the State of New Hampshire shall be entitled to choose three, Massachusetts eight, Rhode Island and Providence Plantations one, Connecticut five, New York six, New Jersey four, Pennsylvania eight, Delaware one, Maryland six, Virginia ten, North Carolina five, South Carolina five and Georgia three.

When vacancies happen in the Representation from any State, the Executive Authority thereof shall issue Writs of Election to fill such Vacancies.

The House of Representatives shall choose their Speaker and other Officers; and shall have the sole Power of Impeachment.

• SECTION 3

The Senate of the United States shall be composed of two Senators from each State, chosen by the Legislature thereof, for six Years; and each Senator shall have one Vote.

Immediately after they shall be assembled in Consequence of the first Election, they shall be divided as equally as may be into three Classes. The Seats of the Senators of the first Class shall be vacated at the Expiration of the second Year, of the second Class at the Expiration of the fourth Year, and of the third Class at the Expiration of the sixth Year, so that one third may be chosen every second Year; and if Vacancies happen by Resignation, or otherwise, during the Recess of the Legislature of any State, the Executive thereof may make temporary Appointments until the next Meeting of the Legislature, which shall then fill such Vacancies.

No person shall be a Senator who shall not have attained to the Age of thirty Years, and been nine Years a Citizen of the United States, and who shall not, when elected, be an Inhabitant of that State for which he shall be chosen.

The Vice President of the United States shall be President of the Senate, but shall have no Vote, unless they be equally divided.

The Senate shall choose their other Officers, and also a President pro tempore, in the absence of the Vice President, or when he shall exercise the Office of President of the United States.

The Senate shall have the sole Power to try all Impeachments. When sitting for that Purpose, they shall be on Oath or Affirmation. When the President of the United States is tried, the Chief Justice shall preside: And no Person shall be convicted without the Concurrence of two thirds of the Members present.

Judgment in Cases of Impeachment shall not extend further than to removal from Office, and disqualification to hold and enjoy any Office of honor, Trust or Profit under the United States: but the Party convicted shall nevertheless be liable and subject to Indictment, Trial, Judgment and Punishment, according to Law.

• SECTION 4

The Times, Places and Manner of holding Elections for Senators and Representatives, shall be prescribed in each State by the Legislature thereof; but the Congress may at any time by Law make or alter such Regulations, except as to the Place of Choosing Senators.

The Congress shall assemble at least once in every Year, and such Meeting shall be on the first Monday in December, unless they shall by Law appoint a different Day.

• SECTION 5

Each House shall be the Judge of the Elections, Returns and Qualifications of its own Members, and a Majority of each shall constitute a Quorum to do Business; but a smaller number may adjourn from day to day, and may be authorized to compel the Attendance of absent Members, in such Manner, and under such Penalties as each House may provide.

Each House may determine the Rules of its Proceedings, punish its Members for disorderly Behavior, and, with the Concurrence of two-thirds, expel a Member.

Each House shall keep a Journal of its Proceedings, and from time to time publish the same, excepting such Parts as may in their Judgment require Secrecy;

and the Yeas and Nays of the Members of either House on any question shall, at the Desire of one fifth of those Present, be entered on the Journal.

Neither House, during the Session of Congress, shall, without the Consent of the other, adjourn for more than three days, nor to any other Place than that in which the two Houses shall be sitting.

• SECTION 6

The Senators and Representatives shall receive a Compensation for their Services, to be ascertained by Law, and paid out of the Treasury of the United States. They shall in all Cases, except Treason, Felony and Breach of the Peace, be privileged from Arrest during their Attendance at the Session of their respective Houses, and in going to and returning from the same; and for any Speech or Debate in either House, they shall not be questioned in any other Place.

No Senator or Representative shall, during the Time for which he was elected, be appointed to any civil Office under the Authority of the United States which shall have been created, or the Emoluments whereof shall have been increased during such time; and no Person holding any Office under the United States, shall be a Member of either House during his Continuance in Office.

• SECTION 7

All bills for raising Revenue shall originate in the House of Representatives; but the Senate may propose or concur with Amendments as on other Bills.

Every Bill which shall have passed the House of Representatives and the Senate, shall, before it become a Law, be presented to the President of the United States. If he approve he shall sign it, but if not he shall return it, with his Objections to that House in which it shall have originated, who shall enter the Objections at large on their Journal, and proceed to reconsider it. If after such Reconsideration two thirds of that House shall agree to pass the Bill, it shall be sent, together with the Objections, to the other House, by which it shall likewise be reconsidered, and if approved by two thirds of that House, it shall become a Law. But in all such Cases the Votes of both Houses shall be determined by Yeas and Nays, and the Names of the Persons voting for and against the Bill shall be entered on the Journal of each House respectively. If any Bill shall not be returned by the President within ten Days (Sundays excepted) after it shall have been presented to him, the Same shall be a Law, in like Manner as if he had signed it, unless the Congress by their Adjournment prevent its Return, in which Case it shall not be a Law.

Every Order, Resolution, or Vote to which the Concurrence of the Senate and House of Representatives may be necessary (except on a question of Adjournment) shall be presented to the President of the United States; and before the Same shall take Effect, shall be approved by him, or being disapproved by him, shall be repassed by two thirds of the Senate and House of Representatives, according to the Rules and Limitations prescribed in the Case of a Bill.

• SECTION 8

The Congress shall have Power to lay and collect Taxes, Duties, Imposts and Excises, to pay the Debts and provide for the common Defence and general Welfare of the United States; but all Duties, Imposts and Excises shall be uniform throughout the United States;

To borrow money on the credit of the United States;

To regulate Commerce with foreign Nations, and among the several States, and with the Indian Tribes;

To establish an uniform Rule of Naturalization, and uniform Laws on the subject of Bankruptcies throughout the United States;

To coin Money, regulate the Value thereof, and of foreign Coin, and fix the Standard of Weights and Measures;

To provide for the Punishment of counterfeiting the Securities and current Coin of the United States;

To establish Post Offices and Post Roads;

To promote the Progress of Science and useful Arts, by securing for limited Times to Authors and Inventors the exclusive Right to their respective Writings and Discoveries;

To constitute Tribunals inferior to the supreme Court;

To define and punish Piracies and Felonies committed on the high Seas, and Offenses against the Law of Nations;

To declare War, grant Letters of Marque and Reprisal, and make Rules concerning Captures on Land and Water;

To raise and support Armies, but no Appropriation of Money to that Use shall be for a longer Term than two Years;

To provide and maintain a Navy;

To make Rules for the Government and Regulation of the land and naval Forces;

To provide for calling forth the Militia to execute the Laws of the Union, suppress Insurrections and repel Invasions;

To provide for organizing, arming, and disciplining the Militia, and for governing such Part of them as may be employed in the Service of the United States, reserving to the States respectively, the Appointment of the Officers, and the Authority of training the Militia according to the discipline prescribed by Congress;

To exercise exclusive Legislation in all Cases whatsoever, over such District (not exceeding ten Miles square) as may, by Cession of particular States, and the acceptance of Congress, become the Seat of the Government of the United States, and to exercise like Authority over all Places purchased by the Consent of the Legislature of the State in which the Same shall be, for the Erection of Forts, Magazines, Arsenals, dock-Yards, and other needful Buildings; and

To make all Laws which shall be necessary and proper for carrying into Execution the foregoing Powers, and all other Powers vested by this Constitution in the Government of the United States, or in any Department or Officer thereof.

• SECTION 9

The Migration or Importation of such Persons as any of the States now existing shall think proper to admit, shall not be prohibited by the Congress prior to the Year one thousand eight hundred and eight, but a tax or duty may be imposed on such Importation, not exceeding ten dollars for each Person.

The privilege of the Writ of Habeas Corpus shall not be suspended, unless when in Cases of Rebellion or Invasion the public Safety may require it.

No Bill of Attainder or ex post facto Law shall be passed.

No capitation, or other direct Tax shall be laid, unless in Proportion to the Census or Enumeration herein before directed to be taken.

No Tax or Duty shall be laid on Articles exported from any State.

No Preference shall be given by any Regulation of Commerce or Revenue to the Ports of one State over those of another; nor shall Vessels bound to, or from, one State, be obliged to enter, clear, or pay Duties in another.

No Money shall be drawn from the Treasury, but in Consequence of Appropriations made by Law; and a regular Statement and Account of the Receipts and Expenditures of all public Money shall be published from time to time.

No Title of Nobility shall be granted by the United States; and no Person holding any Office of Profit or Trust under them, shall, without the Consent of the Congress, accept of any present, Emolument, Office, or Title, of any kind whatever, from any King, Prince or foreign State.

• SECTION 10

No State shall enter into any Treaty, Alliance, or Confederation; grant Letters of Marque and Reprisal; coin Money; emit Bills of Credit; make any Thing but gold and silver Coin a Tender in Payment of Debts; pass any Bill of Attainder, ex post facto Law, or Law impairing the Obligation of Contracts, or grant any Title of Nobility.

No State shall, without the Consent of the Congress, lay any Imposts or Duties on Imports or Exports, except what may be absolutely necessary for executing its inspection Laws; and the net Produce of all Duties and Imposts, laid by any State on Imports or Exports, shall be for the Use of the Treasury of the United States; and all such Laws shall be subject to the Revision and Control of the Congress.

No State shall, without the Consent of Congress, lay any duty of Tonnage, keep Troops, or Ships of War in time of Peace, enter into any Agreement or Compact with another State, or with a foreign Power, or engage in War, unless actually invaded, or in such imminent Danger as will not admit of delay.

ARTICLE 2.

• SECTION I

The executive Power shall be vested in a President of the United States of America. He shall hold his Office during the Term of four Years, and, together with the Vice-President chosen for the same Term, be elected, as follows:

Each State shall appoint, in such Manner as the Legislature thereof may direct, a Number of Electors, equal to the whole Number of Senators and Representatives to which the State may be entitled in the Congress: but no Senator or Representative, or Person holding an Office of Trust or Profit under the United States, shall be appointed an Elector.

The Electors shall meet in their respective States, and vote by Ballot for two persons, of whom one at least shall not be an Inhabitant of the same State with themselves. And they shall make a List of all the Persons voted for, and of the Number of Votes for each; which List they shall sign and certify, and transmit sealed to the Seat of the Government of the United States, directed to the President of the Senate. The President of the Senate shall, in the Presence of the Senate and House of Representatives, open all the

Certificates, and the Votes shall then be counted. The Person having the greatest Number of Votes shall be the President, if such Number be a Majority of the whole Number of Electors appointed; and if there be more than one who have such Majority, and have an equal Number of Votes, then the House of Representatives shall immediately choose by Ballot one of them for President; and if no Person have a Majority, then from the five highest on the List the said House shall in like Manner choose the President. But in choosing the President, the Votes shall be taken by States, the Representation from each State having one Vote; a quorum for this Purpose shall consist of a Member or Members from two-thirds of the States, and a Majority of all the States shall be necessary to a Choice. In every Case, after the Choice of the President, the Person having the greatest Number of Votes of the Electors shall be the Vice President. But if there should remain two or more who have equal Votes, the Senate shall choose from them by Ballot the Vice-President.

The Congress may determine the Time of choosing the Electors, and the Day on which they shall give their Votes; which Day shall be the same throughout the United States.

No person except a natural born Citizen, or a Citizen

of the United States, at the time of the Adoption of this Constitution, shall be eligible to the Office of President; neither shall any Person be eligible to that Office who shall not have attained to the Age of thirty-five Years, and been fourteen Years a Resident within the United States.

In Case of the Removal of the President from Office, or of his Death, Resignation or Inability to discharge the Powers and Duties of the said Office, the same shall devolve on the Vice President, and the Congress may by Law provide for the Case of Removal, Death, Resignation or Inability, both of the President and Vice President, declaring what Officer shall then act as President, and such Officer shall act accordingly, until the Disability be removed, or a President shall be elected.

The President shall, at stated Times, receive for his Services, a Compensation, which shall neither be increased nor diminished during the Period for which he shall have been elected, and he shall not receive within that Period any other Emolument from the United States, or any of them.

Before he enters on the Execution of his Office, he shall take the following Oath or Affirmation:

"I do solemnly swear (or affirm) that I will faithfully execute the Office of President of the United

States, and will to the best of my Ability, preserve, protect and defend the Constitution of the United States."

• SECTION 2

The President shall be Commander in Chief of the Army and Navy of the United States, and of the Militia of the several States, when called into the actual Service of the United States; he may require the Opinion, in writing, of the principal Officer in each of the executive Departments, upon any subject relating to the Duties of their respective Offices, and he shall have Power to Grant Reprieves and Pardons for Offenses against the United States, except in Cases of Impeachment.

He shall have Power, by and with the Advice and Consent of the Senate, to make Treaties, provided two-thirds of the Senators present concur; and he shall nominate, and by and with the Advice and Consent of the Senate, shall appoint Ambassadors, other public Ministers and Consuls, Judges of the supreme Court, and all other Officers of the United States, whose Appointments are not herein otherwise provided for, and which shall be established by Law; but the Congress may by Law vest the Appointment of such inferior Officers, as they think proper, in the

President alone, in the Courts of Law, or in the Heads of Departments.

The President shall have Power to fill up all Vacancies that may happen during the Recess of the Senate, by granting Commissions which shall expire at the End of their next Session.

• SECTION 3

He shall from time to time give to the Congress Information of the State of the Union, and recommend to their Consideration such Measures as he shall judge necessary and expedient; he may, on extraordinary Occasions, convene both Houses, or either of them, and in Case of Disagreement between them, with Respect to the Time of Adjournment, he may adjourn them to such Time as he shall think proper; he shall receive Ambassadors and other public Ministers; he shall take Care that the Laws be faithfully executed, and shall Commission all the Officers of the United States.

• SECTION 4

The President, Vice President and all civil Officers of the United States, shall be removed from Office on Impeachment for, and Conviction of, Treason, Bribery, or other high Crimes and Misdemeanors.

ARTICLE 3.

- SECTION I

The judicial Power of the United States, shall be vested in one supreme Court, and in such inferior Courts as the Congress may from time to time ordain and establish. The Judges, both of the supreme and inferior Courts, shall hold their Offices during good Behavior, and shall, at stated Times, receive for their Services a Compensation which shall not be diminished during their Continuance in Office.

- SECTION 2

The judicial Power shall extend to all Cases, in Law and Equity, arising under this Constitution, the Laws of the United States, and Treaties made, or which shall be made, under their Authority; to all Cases affecting Ambassadors, other public Ministers and Consuls; to all Cases of admiralty and maritime Jurisdiction; to Controversies to which the United States shall be a Party; to Controversies between two or more States; between a State and Citizens of another State; between Citizens of different States; between Citizens of the same State claiming Lands under Grants of different

States; and between a State, or the Citizens thereof, and foreign States, Citizens or Subjects.

In all Cases affecting Ambassadors, other public Ministers and Consuls, and those in which a State shall be Party, the supreme Court shall have original Jurisdiction. In all the other Cases before mentioned, the supreme Court shall have appellate Jurisdiction, both as to Law and Fact, with such Exceptions, and under such Regulations as the Congress shall make.

The Trial of all Crimes, except in Cases of Impeachment, shall be by Jury; and such Trial shall be held in the State where the said Crimes shall have been committed; but when not committed within any State, the Trial shall be at such Place or Places as the Congress may by Law have directed.

• SECTION 3

Treason against the United States, shall consist only in levying War against them, or in adhering to their Enemies, giving them Aid and Comfort. No Person shall be convicted of Treason unless on the Testimony of two Witnesses to the same overt Act, or on Confession in open Court.

The Congress shall have power to declare the Punishment of Treason, but no Attainder of Treason shall work Corruption of Blood, or Forfeiture, except during the Life of the Person attainted.

ARTICLE 4.

• SECTION 1

Full Faith and Credit shall be given in each State to the public Acts, Records, and judicial Proceedings of every other State. And the Congress may by general Laws prescribe the Manner in which such Acts, Records and Proceedings shall be proved, and the Effect thereof.

• SECTION 2

The Citizens of each State shall be entitled to all Privileges and Immunities of Citizens in the several States.

A Person charged in any State with Treason, Felony, or other Crime, who shall flee from Justice, and be found in another State, shall on demand of the executive Authority of the State from which he fled, be delivered up, to be removed to the State having Jurisdiction of the Crime.

No Person held to Service or Labour in one State, under the Laws thereof, escaping into another, shall, in Consequence of any Law or Regulation therein, be discharged from such Service or Labour, but shall be delivered up on Claim of the Party to whom such Service or Labour may be due.

• SECTION 3

New States may be admitted by the Congress into this Union; but no new States shall be formed or erected within the Jurisdiction of any other State; nor any State be formed by the Junction of two or more States, or parts of States, without the Consent of the Legislatures of the States concerned as well as of the Congress.

The Congress shall have Power to dispose of and make all needful Rules and Regulations respecting the Territory or other Property belonging to the United States; and nothing in this Constitution shall be so construed as to Prejudice any Claims of the United States, or of any particular State.

• SECTION 4

The United States shall guarantee to every State in this Union a Republican Form of Government, and shall protect each of them against Invasion; and on Application of the Legislature, or of the Executive (when the Legislature cannot be convened) against domestic Violence.

ARTICLE 5.

The Congress, whenever two-thirds of both Houses shall deem it necessary, shall propose Amendments to this Constitution, or, on the Application of the Legislatures of two-thirds of the several States, shall call a Convention for proposing Amendments, which, in either Case, shall be valid to all Intents and Purposes, as part of this Constitution, when ratified by the Legislatures of three-fourths of the several States, or by Conventions in three-fourths thereof, as the one or the other Mode of Ratification may be proposed by the Congress; provided that no Amendment which may be made prior to the Year one thousand eight hundred and eight shall in any Manner affect the first and fourth Clauses in the Ninth Section of the First Article; and that no State, without its Consent, shall be deprived of its equal Suffrage in the Senate.

ARTICLE 6.

All Debts contracted and Engagements entered into, before the Adoption of this Constitution, shall be as valid against the United States under this Constitution, as under the Confederation.

This Constitution, and the Laws of the United States which shall be made in Pursuance thereof, and all Treaties made, or which shall be made, under the Authority of the United States, shall be the supreme Law of the Land; and the Judges in every State shall be bound thereby, any Thing in the Constitution or Laws of any State to the Contrary notwithstanding.

The Senators and Representatives before mentioned, and the Members of the several State Legislatures, and all executive and judicial Officers, both of the United States and of the several States, shall be bound by Oath or Affirmation, to support this Constitution; but no religious Test shall ever be required as a Qualification to any Office or public Trust under the United States.

ARTICLE 7.

The Ratification of the Conventions of nine States, shall be sufficient for the Establishment of this Constitution between the States so ratifying the same.

Done in Convention by the Unanimous Consent of the States present the Seventeenth Day of September in the Year of our Lord one thousand seven hundred and eighty-seven, and of the Independence of the United States of America the Twelfth. In Witness whereof We have hereunto subscribed our Names.

George Washington: PRESIDENT AND DEPUTY FROM VIRGINIA

NEW HAMPSHIRE: *John Langdon, Nicholas Gilman*

MASSACHUSETTS: *Nathaniel Gorham, Rufus King*

CONNECTICUT: *William Samuel Johnson, Roger Sherman*

NEW YORK: *Alexander Hamilton*

NEW JERSEY: *William Livingston, David Brearley, William Paterson, Jonathan Dayton*

PENNSYLVANIA: *Benjamin Franklin, Thomas Mifflin, Robert Morris, George Clymer, Thomas Fitzsimons, Jared Ingersoll, James Wilson, Gouvernour Morris*

DELAWARE: *George Read, Gunning Bedford, Jr., John Dickinson, Richard Bassett, Jacob Broom*

MARYLAND: *James McHenry, Daniel of St. Thomas Jenifer, Daniel Carroll*

VIRGINIA: *John Blair, James Madison, Jr.*

NORTH CAROLINA: *William Blount, Richard Dobbs Spaight, Hugh Williamson*

SOUTH CAROLINA: *John Rutledge, Charles Cotesworth Pinckney, Charles Pinckney, Pierce Butler*

GEORGIA: *William Few, Abraham Baldwin*

Attest: *William Jackson*, Secretary

• AMENDMENT 1 •

Congress shall make no law respecting an establishment of religion, or prohibiting the free exercise thereof; or abridging the freedom of speech, or of the press; or the right of the people peaceably to assemble, and to petition the Government for a redress of grievances.

• AMENDMENT 2 •

A well regulated Militia, being necessary to the security of a free State, the right of the people to keep and bear Arms, shall not be infringed.

• AMENDMENT 3 •

No Soldier shall, in time of peace, be quartered in any house, without the consent of the Owner, nor in time of war, but in a manner to be prescribed by law.

• AMENDMENT 4 •

The right of the people to be secure in their persons, houses, papers, and effects, against unreasonable searches and seizures, shall not be violated, and no Warrants shall issue, but upon probable cause, supported by Oath or affirmation, and particularly describing the place to be searched, and the persons or things to be seized.

• AMENDMENT 5 •

No person shall be held to answer for a capital, or otherwise infamous crime, unless on a presentment or indictment of a Grand Jury, except in cases arising in the land or naval forces, or in the Militia, when in actual service in time of War or public danger; nor shall any person be subject for the same offense to be twice put in jeopardy of life or limb; nor shall he be compelled in any criminal case to be a witness against himself, nor be deprived of life, liberty, or property, without due process of law; nor shall private property be taken for public use, without just compensation.

· AMENDMENT 6 ·

In all criminal prosecutions, the accused shall enjoy the right to a speedy and public trial, by an impartial jury of the State and district wherein the crime shall have been committed, which district shall have been previously ascertained by law, and to be informed of the nature and cause of the accusation; to be confronted with the witnesses against him; to have compulsory process for obtaining witnesses in his favor, and to have the Assistance of Counsel for his defence.

• AMENDMENT 7 •

In Suits at common law, where the value in controversy shall exceed twenty dollars, the right of trial by jury shall be preserved, and no fact tried by a jury, shall be otherwise re-examined in any Court of the United States, than according to the rules of the common law.

• AMENDMENT 8 •

Excessive bail shall not be required, nor excessive fines imposed, nor cruel and unusual punishments inflicted.

• AMENDMENT 9 •

The enumeration in the Constitution, of certain rights, shall not be construed to deny or disparage others retained by the people.

• AMENDMENT 10 •

The powers not delegated to the United States by the Constitution, nor prohibited by it to the States, are reserved to the States respectively, or to the people.

• AMENDMENT 11 •

The Judicial power of the United States shall not be construed to extend to any suit in law or equity, commenced or prosecuted against one of the United States by Citizens of another State, or by Citizens or Subjects of any Foreign State.

• AMENDMENT 12 •

The Electors shall meet in their respective states, and vote by ballot for President and Vice-President, one of whom, at least, shall not be an inhabitant of the same state with themselves; they shall name in their ballots the person voted for as President, and in distinct ballots the person voted for as Vice-President, and they shall make distinct lists of all persons voted for as President, and of all persons voted for as Vice-President, and of the number of votes for each, which lists they shall sign and certify, and transmit sealed to the seat of the government of the United States, directed to the President of the Senate;

The President of the Senate shall, in the presence of the Senate and House of Representatives, open all the certificates and the votes shall then be counted;

The person having the greatest Number of votes for

President, shall be the President, if such number be a majority of the whole number of Electors appointed; and if no person have such majority, then from the persons having the highest numbers not exceeding three on the list of those voted for as President, the House of Representatives shall choose immediately, by ballot, the President. But in choosing the President, the votes shall be taken by states, the representation from each state having one vote; a quorum for this purpose shall consist of a member or members from two-thirds of the states, and a majority of all the states shall be necessary to a choice. And if the House of Representatives shall not choose a President whenever the right of choice shall devolve upon them, before the fourth day of March next following, then the Vice-President shall act as President, as in the case of the death or other constitutional disability of the President.

The person having the greatest number of votes as Vice-President, shall be the Vice-President, if such number be a majority of the whole number of Electors appointed, and if no person have a majority, then from the two highest numbers on the list, the Senate shall choose the Vice-President; a quorum for the purpose shall consist of two-thirds of the whole number of Senators, and a majority of the whole number shall be necessary to a choice. But no person constitutionally ineligible to the office of President shall be eligible to that of Vice-President of the United States.

• AMENDMENT 13 •

1. Neither slavery nor involuntary servitude, except as a punishment for crime whereof the party shall have been duly convicted, shall exist within the United States, or any place subject to their jurisdiction.

2. Congress shall have power to enforce this article by appropriate legislation.

• AMENDMENT 14 •

1. All persons born or naturalized in the United States, and subject to the jurisdiction thereof, are citizens of the United States and of the State wherein they reside. No State shall make or enforce any law which shall abridge the privileges or immunities of citizens of the United States; nor shall any State deprive any person of life, liberty, or property, without due process of law; nor deny to any person within its jurisdiction the equal protection of the laws.

2. Representatives shall be apportioned among the several States according to their respective numbers,

counting the whole number of persons in each State, excluding Indians not taxed. But when the right to vote at any election for the choice of electors for President and Vice-President of the United States, Representatives in Congress, the Executive and Judicial officers of a State, or the members of the Legislature thereof, is denied to any of the male inhabitants of such State, being twenty-one years of age, and citizens of the United States, or in any way abridged, except for participation in rebellion, or other crime, the basis of representation therein shall be reduced in the proportion which the number of such male citizens shall bear to the whole number of male citizens twenty-one years of age in such State.

3. No person shall be a Senator or Representative in Congress, or elector of President and Vice-President, or hold any office, civil or military, under the United States, or under any State, who, having previously taken an oath, as a member of Congress, or as an officer of the United States, or as a member of any State legislature, or as an executive or judicial officer of any State, to support the Constitution of the United States, shall have engaged in insurrection or rebellion against the same, or given aid or comfort to the enemies thereof. But Congress may by a vote of two-thirds of each House, remove such disability.

4. The validity of the public debt of the United States, authorized by law, including debts incurred for payment of pensions and bounties for services in suppressing insurrection or rebellion, shall not be questioned. But neither the United States nor any State shall assume or pay any debt or obligation incurred in aid of insurrection or rebellion against the United States, or any claim for the loss or emancipation of any slave; but all such debts, obligations and claims shall be held illegal and void.

5. The Congress shall have power to enforce, by appropriate legislation, the provisions of this article.

• AMENDMENT 15 •

1. The right of citizens of the United States to vote shall not be denied or abridged by the United States or by any State on account of race, color, or previous condition of servitude.

2. The Congress shall have power to enforce this article by appropriate legislation.

• AMENDMENT 16 •

The Congress shall have power to lay and collect taxes on incomes, from whatever source derived, without apportionment among the several States, and without regard to any census or enumeration.

• AMENDMENT 17 •

The Senate of the United States shall be composed of two Senators from each State, elected by the people thereof, for six years; and each Senator shall have one vote. The electors in each State shall have the qualifications requisite for electors of the most numerous branch of the State legislatures.

When vacancies happen in the representation of any State in the Senate, the executive authority of such State shall issue writs of election to fill such vacancies: Provided that the legislature of any State may empower the executive thereof to make temporary appointments until the people fill the vacancies by election as the legislature may direct.

This amendment shall not be so construed as to affect the election or term of any Senator chosen before it becomes valid as part of the Constitution.

• AMENDMENT 18 •

1. After one year from the ratification of this article, the manufacture, sale or transportation of intoxicating

liquors within, the importation thereof into, or the exportation thereof from the United States and all territory subject to the jurisdiction thereof for beverage purposes is hereby prohibited.

2. The Congress and the several States shall have concurrent power to enforce this article by appropriate legislation.

3. This article shall be inoperative unless it shall have been ratified as an amendment to the Constitution by the legislatures of the several States, as provided in the Constitution, within seven years from the date of the submission hereof to the States by the Congress.

• AMENDMENT 19 •

The right of citizens of the United States to vote shall not be denied or abridged by the United States or by any State on account of sex.

Congress shall have power to enforce this article by appropriate legislation.

• AMENDMENT 20 •

1. The terms of the President and Vice President shall end at noon on the 20th day of January, and the

terms of Senators and Representatives at noon on the 3d day of January, of the years in which such terms would have ended if this article had not been ratified; and the terms of their successors shall then begin.

2. The Congress shall assemble at least once in every year, and such meeting shall begin at noon on the 3d day of January, unless they shall by law appoint a different day.

3. If, at the time fixed for the beginning of the term of the President, the President elect shall have died, the Vice President elect shall become President. If a President shall not have been chosen before the time fixed for the beginning of his term, or if the President elect shall have failed to qualify, then the Vice President elect shall act as President until a President shall have qualified; and the Congress may by law provide for the case wherein neither a President elect nor a Vice President elect shall have qualified, declaring who shall then act as President, or the manner in which one who is to act shall be selected, and such person shall act accordingly until a President or Vice President shall have qualified.

4. The Congress may by law provide for the case of the death of any of the persons from whom the House of Representatives may choose a President whenever the right of choice shall have devolved upon them,

and for the case of the death of any of the persons from whom the Senate may choose a Vice President whenever the right of choice shall have devolved upon them.

5. Sections 1 and 2 shall take effect on the 15th day of October following the ratification of this article.

6. This article shall be inoperative unless it shall have been ratified as an amendment to the Constitution by the legislatures of three-fourths of the several States within seven years from the date of its submission.

• AMENDMENT 21 •

1. The eighteenth article of amendment to the Constitution of the United States is hereby repealed.

2. The transportation or importation into any State, Territory, or possession of the United States for delivery or use therein of intoxicating liquors, in violation of the laws thereof, is hereby prohibited.

3. The article shall be inoperative unless it shall have been ratified as an amendment to the Constitution by conventions in the several States, as provided in the Constitution, within seven years from the date of the submission hereof to the States by the Congress.

• AMENDMENT 22 •

1. No person shall be elected to the office of the President more than twice, and no person who has held the office of President, or acted as President, for more than two years of a term to which some other person was elected President shall be elected to the office of the President more than once. But this Article shall not apply to any person holding the office of President, when this Article was proposed by the Congress, and shall not prevent any person who may be holding the office of President, or acting as President, during the term within which this Article becomes operative from holding the office of President or acting as President during the remainder of such term.

2. This article shall be inoperative unless it shall have been ratified as an amendment to the Constitution by the legislatures of three-fourths of the several States within seven years from the date of its submission to the States by the Congress.

• AMENDMENT 23 •

1. The District constituting the seat of Government of the United States shall appoint in such manner as

the Congress may direct: A number of electors of President and Vice President equal to the whole number of Senators and Representatives in Congress to which the District would be entitled if it were a State, but in no event more than the least populous State; they shall be in addition to those appointed by the States, but they shall be considered, for the purposes of the election of President and Vice President, to be electors appointed by a State; and they shall meet in the District and perform such duties as provided by the twelfth article of amendment.

2. The Congress shall have power to enforce this article by appropriate legislation.

• AMENDMENT 24 •

1. The right of citizens of the United States to vote in any primary or other election for President or Vice President, for electors for President or Vice President, or for Senator or Representative in Congress, shall not be denied or abridged by the United States or any State by reason of failure to pay any poll tax or other tax.

2. The Congress shall have power to enforce this article by appropriate legislation.

• AMENDMENT 25 •

1. In case of the removal of the President from office or of his death or resignation, the Vice President shall become President.

2. Whenever there is a vacancy in the office of the Vice President, the President shall nominate a Vice President who shall take office upon confirmation by a majority vote of both Houses of Congress.

3. Whenever the President transmits to the President pro tempore of the Senate and the Speaker of the House of Representatives his written declaration that he is unable to discharge the powers and duties of his office, and until he transmits to them a written declaration to the contrary, such powers and duties shall be discharged by the Vice President as Acting President.

4. Whenever the Vice President and a majority of either the principal officers of the executive departments or of such other body as Congress may by law provide, transmit to the President pro tempore of the Senate and the Speaker of the House of Representatives their written declaration that the President is unable to discharge the powers and duties of his office, the Vice President shall immediately assume the powers and duties of the office as Acting President.

Thereafter, when the President transmits to the

President pro tempore of the Senate and the Speaker of the House of Representatives his written declaration that no inability exists, he shall resume the powers and duties of his office unless the Vice President and a majority of either the principal officers of the executive department or of such other body as Congress may by law provide, transmit within four days to the President pro tempore of the Senate and the Speaker of the House of Representatives their written declaration that the President is unable to discharge the powers and duties of his office. Thereupon Congress shall decide the issue, assembling within forty-eight hours for that purpose if not in session. If the Congress, within twenty-one days after receipt of the latter written declaration, or, if Congress is not in session, within twenty-one days after Congress is required to assemble, determines by two-thirds vote of both Houses that the President is unable to discharge the powers and duties of his office, the Vice President shall continue to discharge the same as Acting President; otherwise, the President shall resume the powers and duties of his office.

• AMENDMENT 26 •

1. The right of citizens of the United States, who are eighteen years of age or older, to vote shall not be denied or abridged by the United States or by any State on account of age.

2. The Congress shall have power to enforce this article by appropriate legislation.

• AMENDMENT 27 •

No law, varying the compensation for the services of the Senators and Representatives, shall take effect, until an election of Representatives shall have intervened.

BIBLIOGRAPHY

Bloom, Allan. The Closing of the American Mind. New York: Simon & Schuster, 1987.

Bloom examines how modern American universities' abandonment of the traditional liberal arts curriculum, and the influence of Germanic nihilism, homogenized and depressed the culture of America's educated class.

Bork, Robert H. *The Tempting of America: The Political Seduction of the Law*. New York: Touchstone,1990.

Robert Bork's history of judicial activism in America shows how political elites have turned the courts into tools for enacting changes that the American people reject. Denying the validity of the Constitution as it was written, they have created one that they can mold and change as they see fit.

Buckley, William F. *God and Man at Yale: The Superstitions of "Academic Freedom."* Washington D.C.: Henry Regnery Company, 1951.

William F. Buckley here exposes the disregard and contempt that many academics show towards traditional American moral and political values and for the American people in general.

Burnham, James. *The Managerial Revolution: What Is Happening in the World*. 1940.

In this book which inspired George Orwell's famous novel *1984*, Burnham discusses the rise of a managerial class specially trained in the organization and administration of businesses and government. As the social and economic spheres grow increasingly more complex, these managers monopolize the ownership of information and use it for their own ends, transforming into a sort of ruling class and effecting a revolution in society as a whole.

Codevilla, Angelo M. *The Character of Nations*. New York: Basics Books, 2009.

This book shows how regimes—governments plus elites—affect peoples' capacity for prosperity, civility, family, and spiritual life. Its discussion of America shows how the choices we make about public policy shape our own character.

George, Robert P. *The Clash of Orthodoxies: Law, Religion, and Morality in Crisis*. Wilmington, DE: ISI Books, 2001.

Professor Robert George shows that American concepts of freedom and equality are inseparable from our Judeo-Christian roots and bound up with reason. George shows that Judeo-Christian beliefs are rationally superior to modern secular liberal ones. Orthodox secularism, what America's ruling class is educated in, is simply not a substantial rebuke to traditional Judeo-Christian teachings.

Goldberg, Jonah. *Liberal Fascism: The Secret History of the American Left, from Mussolini to the Politics of Change.* New York: Doubleday, 2008.

Goldberg shows that European fascism and American progressivism share the same intellectual roots.

Hayek, Friedrich. *The Road to Serfdom.*

Few books are more important or relevant than Friedrich von Hayek's first classic *The Road to Serfdom*. It shows that all forms of centralized economic planning invariably lead to the expansion of arbitrary state power. Centralized economic planning and "rule" by experts, according to Hayek, fertilize the seed of totalitarianism.

Kirk, Russell. *The Roots of American Order.* 1974.

Kirk argues that American Order is grounded in certain permanent institutions, beliefs, and characteristics of Americans: that to restore liberty to its rightful place in society, we must strengthen the foundations on which it is built: the habits of heart and mind that make America exceptional.

Lerner, Robert, Althea Nagai, and Stanley Rothman. *American Elites*. New Haven: Yale University Press, 1996.

According to "the most comprehensive survey ever conducted on elite groups in the U.S." America's ruling class is neither more informed nor more intellectually rigorous than any other class in American society. Lerner and Nagai uncover a usually unchallenged set of orthodoxies, adherence to which alienates America's Liberal elites from the rest of the country. Realizing their alienation they seek the transformation of American society through non-democratic means.

Levin, Mark R. *Liberty and Tyranny: A Conservative Manifesto*. New York: Simon & Schuster, 2009.

In his New York Times bestseller, Mr. Levin attacks American liberalism and calls for a renewed understanding of core American principles. He argues that core conservative philosophical principles are the best defense against tyrannical government.

Locke, John. *Two Treatises of Government*. Ed. Peter Laslett. New York: Cambridge University Press, 1988.

John Locke's *Two Treatises* provided much of the foundational thought for the American Revolution, clearly delineating the natural rights of life, liberty, and property that would so greatly influence the Founding Fathers. The first treatise refuted the "divine right of kings," clearing the way for a theory of government based on the social contract and the rights of the individual.

Marini, John and Ken Masugi, Eds. *The Progressive Revolution in Politics and Political Science: Transforming the American Regime*. Lanham, MD: Rowman and Littlefield, 2005.

This book's several essays discuss the progressive movement's conflict with the principles of the American Founding, particularly the concepts of Nature and natural rights.

Meese, Edwin, Matthew Spalding, and David Forte, eds. *The Heritage Guide to the Constitution*. Washington DC: The Heritage Foundation, 2005.

This guide provides an analysis of each clause in the Constitution, as well as key court cases and documents essential to understanding the Constitution. In an era of heated constitutional debate, this book gives guidance and clarity to any reader on the meaning of America's founding charter.

Neuhaus, Richard John. *The Naked Public Square: Religion and Democracy in America*. 1984.

Richard John Neuhaus shows how the US government's rejection of religion as the ethical standard of public life has contributed to the erosion of the American family and social institutions.

Pestritto, Ronald. *Woodrow Wilson and the Roots of Modern Liberalism*. Lanham, MD: Rowman and Littlefield, 2005.

In this book, Pestritto examines Wilson's writings and speeches and explains how he and progressivism reshaped 20th century American government.

Publius. *The Federalist Papers*. Ed. Clinton Rossiter. New York: New American Library, 1999.

This timeless collection of essays written by Alexander Hamilton, James Madison, and John Jay, provides valuable insight into the intention and purpose of the Constitution and its Framers. Written in advocacy of the new Constitution during its ratification period, these essays explain what the Constitution is and the vision that guided its creation.

Spalding, Matthew. *We Still Hold These Truths: Rediscovering Our Principles, Reclaiming Our Future*. Wilmington, DE: ISI Books, 2009.

This book looks at ten core principles that shaped the American founding, such as free enterprise and the rule of law, how America has moved away from those principles, and what we must do to renew the Founder's vision for America.

Watson, Bradley C.S. *Living Constitution, Dying Faith: Progressivism and the New Science of Jurisprudence*. Wilmington, DE: ISI Books 2009.

Watson investigates the contemporary notion of the Constitution as a living organism and shows this to be a radical departure from limited constitutional government as such.

Weaver, Richard M. *Ideas Have Consequences*. 1948.

This book outlines the ideas which American universities have inculcated uniformly into two generations, the consequence of which is a corrupt ruling class.

Wilson, James Q. *Bureaucracy: What Government Agencies Do and Why They Do It*. New York: Basic Books, 1989.

This book represents the comprehensive guide to government bureaucracy the different categories of governmental agencies, their administrators, their operations, their organization, their motives and interests, and their political context.

ABOUT THE AUTHOR

ANGELO M. CODEVILLA is professor emeritus of
international relations at Boston University. Educated
at Rutgers (1965), Notre Dame (1968), and the Cla-
remont graduate university (1973), Codevilla served
in the U.S. Navy, the U.S. Foreign Service, and on
the U.S. Senate Select Committee on Intelligence. He
taught philosophy at Georgetown, classified intelligence matters at the U.S. Naval Postgraduate School.
During a decade at Stanford's Hoover Institution, he
wrote books on war, intelligence, and the character
of nations. At Boston University, he taught international relations from the perspectives of history and
character. His latest book is *Advice to War Presidents*
(Basic Books 2009).